Christian
Parenting

Christian Parenting

BETSY DAWN INSKEEP SMYLIE
JOHN SHERIDAN SMYLIE

UPPER
ROOM BOOKS
NASHVILLE

CHRISTIAN PARENTING.
©1991 by Betsy Dawn Inskeep Smylie and John Sheridan Smylie.
All rights reserved.

No part of this book may be used or reproduced in any manner
whatsoever without permission except in the case of brief
quotations embodied in critical articles or reviews.
For information address: THE UPPER ROOM, 1908 Grand Avenue,
Post Office Box 189, Nashville, Tennessee 37202.

Scripture quotations are from the REVISED STANDARD VERSION of the
Bible, copyright 1946, 1952, 1971 by the Division of Christian
Education of the National Council of Churches in the USA.
Used by permission.

Cover design: Jane Word.
Cover photograph by Karina McDaniel, State of Tennessee.

Printed in the United States of America.
First printing: October, 1991 (5).

ISBN 0-8358-0642-1
Library of Congress Catalog Card Number: 91-65727

To
Shemaleiah Dawn Smylie
and
Nathan John Smylie

Preface

WE ARE BOTH EPISCOPAL PRIESTS. We met and married in
an Episcopal monastery during our seminary years. We
started our family a year later, before either of us was
ordained. Even then, we somehow had the sense that God
would use our children to shape and form us as much as he
would work through the vocation to which we were called.

Our daughter Shemaleiah was born while we were still
in school. She attended graduate school seminars when she
was a week old, nestled in her mother's front pack, close to
the milk supply. Before the age of two she was correcting her
parents. Her father had emphasized speaking clearly and
correctly, saying yes rather than yeah. At the dinner table

one evening when a yeah slipped out, she turned to her father and said, "Daddy, you mean yes." We both knew then that we were in for it, that this parenting business was a two-way street.

Nathan arrived in our family when John had his first parish and Betsy was filling in for clergy on vacations. The obstetrician at the Roman Catholic hospital had never encountered a priest couple like us and at crucial times in the delivery would say, "Push, Rev, push."

Nathan was born deaf, though it took us a while to figure that out. His heightened sense of the visual has opened up a new perspective to us. His first word in sign language was "light," and while his older sister would conk out in her car seat on family trips, the darkness would energize Nathan, who would stay awake for hours checking out the street lights and waking up his mom to tell her which ones were broken.

This book began to take form at a time in the life of our church when issues of human sexuality were being bitterly debated. While not denying the importance of facing and struggling with hard and sensitive issues, we grew weary of the negativity and sensationalism surrounding such discussions and longed to speak of the simple and ordinary ways we were discovering God in the midst of our family.

John, the dreamer, the poet, thought we should work on a book together. Betsy, the prose writer, the scholar, thought that was crazy, that only experts who had done years of research should venture to write a book. John persisted. Betsy balked, until a trip to her hometown brought a chance meeting with her fourth grade teacher who said to her, "Have you written a book yet?" As is often the case, it took someone far away to open her eyes to the suggestion she had been hearing close at home.

We started working, brainstorming together, shaping

the chapters, digging into the scriptures, telling stories. We were amazed and grateful that the very process itself opened us to experience God's grace in the midst of some very rocky times. It reminded us again and again that we were not experts on parenting or any other family issues for that matter, and that we needed to hear the message of forgiveness, of hope, of God's real and lively presence in our family. We offer this book in hopes that it will be a vehicle of God's grace to other families who struggle to be faithful.

&

We especially want to thank our parents, Donald W. Inskeep, Elizabeth D. Inskeep, Charles A. Smylie, and Marguerette S. Smylie who nurtured us in homes where we experienced the love of God and the strong bonds of family. We thank Sharon Bowles from Christ Church, Stanhope, New Jersey, who spent endless hours with our family in healing prayer at the time this book was unfolding. We thank Tanner Gay, whose red pencil aided us enormously in the initial preparation of the manuscript.

And we thank the people of God who have lovingly supported our family through the years, especially those of the Society of Saint John the Evangelist in Cambridge, Massachusetts; St. Mary's in Sparta, New Jersey; Calvary in Summit, New Jersey; St. Thomas in Vernon, New Jersey; Ephphatha Church of the Deaf in Western, New York; and Trinity Church of Hamburg, New York.

One

Saying Yes to the Journey

A FRIEND CAME TO US ONE EVENING for counsel and support. He was a brand-new father and was very excited about his new little daughter. He had coached his wife through a lengthy labor and delivery, and they were proud and satisfied as a new family. But the baby's incessant crying was driving him crazy. He knew that some babies were just criers, that you do your best to take care of their needs and wait it out, hoping they will pass through the stage quickly. But he was unable to be rational and objective in his own situation. Her crying had touched off something in him that made him want to run away, and he was troubled by these feelings.

As we talked and prayed together, it became clear to us that the crying of his baby had brought to the surface many unrecognized childhood needs that our friend had failed to see and acknowledge before now. His parents had been harsh and demanding professionals, never satisfied with his performance, and never having the time to give him the love and affirmation that he needed. His newborn's crying had awakened in him a sense of his own unmet needs which now seemed so overwhelming that he just wanted to escape. As he consciously and prayerfully began to bring his needy heart into God's presence and to experience the unconditional love and acceptance of God's grace, he was able to accept and embrace his daughter when she cried.

The journey and adventure of parenting is filled with experiences that touch the deep places of our hearts and expose our most hidden vulnerabilities.

Where does a mother go when she knows that once more she has lost the ability to control not only her children, but her own tongue and temper? Where does a father go when, after comforting his child in the darkness, he faces his own inner fears and darkness and can find no one to chase away the bogeyman?

Who parents the *parents*? Who holds *them* in the darkness? Who accepts *them* in their rage? Who picks up the pieces after their broken attempts at being the kind of parent they had always thought they should be? Who binds up their wounds and gives them the courage to keep at it?

&

The living Christ longs to be present in the deep moments of need that are evident in any family. This book is an invitation to you to open yourself and the life of your family to that living and healing presence of Christ. We invite you to come along with us as we experience the power of Christ to heal, deliver, and set free. And we invite you to open yourself to experience that wonderful ministry in your family today.

Each chapter in this book starts with a theoretical section to lay a foundation for further reflection. Then follows a biblical section that highlights Jesus' ministry among individuals and families. Finally, through story and specific suggestions, we make practical applications for contemporary family life.

However, this is not a psychological self-help book filled with good ideas about how to improve your family life. Rather, it is an invitation to believe that God is present in the midst of your family and calling you to join in the work being done there.

All too often we think that we need to know and fully understand God's ways before we will venture to walk in them. We want a nice, neat system of spiritual principles by which we can control how and when God is allowed to get involved with us and our families. But God is forever breaking out of those boxes we build, shattering our expectations and hopes for order and security, and calling us to welcome the new and unexpected ways God works in our lives.

&

Think of Mary and Joseph.

They were a devout and eager young couple, very much longing to commit their upcoming marriage and life together to the religious principles that had nurtured them. Then an angelic visitor brought the startling news that Mary is to bear the long-awaited Messiah, and that the baby is to be conceived not by Joseph, but by the Holy Spirit. Such unsettling news totally shattered any hopes for the quiet and idyllic life they had imagined together. Separately and alone, they each had the opportunity to say yes to God's new and amazing presence in their midst. Because they said yes, the future of their family life, as well as the future of life on our planet, was radically changed. Because they dared to believe first, even that which defied understanding, they were able to bring the living Christ to birth in their midst.

We invite you to join in the wonderful and difficult adventure of believing in Christ and joining with him as he is present in your family.

Perhaps you are a devoted Christian with some fairly strong ideas of what God expects of you as a Christian family. Perhaps you are filled with guilt and resentment because in some way your family falls short of the shining Christian ideal you feel judged by. Perhaps you are struggling with divorce, substance abuse, special-needs children, financial insecurity, or other difficulties that cause you to feel isolated and abandoned by the faith community. Perhaps you do not even know if you believe anything at all anymore. Perhaps you are wondering what God might have to do with your family and are intrigued enough to do a little exploring with us. At whatever point we find ourselves, Jesus comes, inviting us to lay down our preconceptions, inviting us to give up the game of trying to figure it all out beforehand in order to control the experience, inviting us to say yes to journey with him.

May God bless you on your journey!

Two

In the Midst of the Ordinary

OURS IS A CULTURE TYRANNIZED BY TIME. Our network of instant communications with the world, our sophisticated modes of travel, and our timesaving devices, from computers to microwave ovens, have given us the illusion that our time and opportunities are limitless. In our frantic struggle to cram all that we want into our lifestyles, we very often lose touch with the ability to be alert and attentive to the present moment.

When we were new parents, some older and wiser friends took us aside and did their best to dispel the myth of "quality time." They agreed that children need quality time, with close attention and interest in what they are doing along with a parent's mere bodily presence with them. But they also told us that children need a large dose of "quantity time" as well. They need to know that we are there and available for them, that they have a high priority amidst the demands and challenges of our lives.

Each of us must work out the delicate balance between work and home with much care, aware that the things that our culture values—career advancement, financial success—are not necessarily at the top of God's list of eternal values. So often we feel that the most important thing we can give to our children is economic security and all the good gifts and opportunities that money can bring. Certainly, it is our responsibility to work hard to provide for our children, but perhaps their need for our loving presence runs deeper than their material requirements.

To give our attention to others is a very real gift. It affirms that their being is valuable to us, that they are a unique gift from God to us.

Mother Teresa, who amazes this world with the extravagance of her love and devotion to the poorest of the poor, credits her astounding impact to a very simple truth. She sees each and every one, from the abandoned newborn to the dying victim of the slums, as Jesus sees them, with eyes of love, as valuable creatures made in the image of God.

How transforming it would be to our daily routine if we were to see each interchange with our children as an opportunity to serve God's most precious creatures. To do so, we must free ourselves from the encumbrances of worries about the past and the future. We cannot fully listen to an account of a crisis on the playground or genuinely admire a new artistic creation if we are mentally rehashing a difficult conversation at the office or planning the grocery list for the next day.

C. S. Lewis says that the only point at which time intersects eternity is in the present moment. When we become bogged down in regrets or grudges from the past or caught up in worries or fantasies about the future, we remove ourselves from the only opportunity we have to touch God's eternal kingdom.

This misuse of time is a problem that many of us have had long before we had children. We have come to see it as a simple issue of control and trust. For some, agonizing over the past or worrying about the future is a way of masking and controlling the pain in our lives. Being wide open to the present moment seems to leave us just too vulnerable, so we attempt to control the uncertainty by rehashing and rehearsing. It is the old, "Expect the worst, so at least you will be prepared" mind set. It is a mind set that wreaks havoc on the spirit whether one has children or not. It closes down the opportunity for delight, wonder, and playfulness. It does the same to the chance to experience real feelings in the here and now, whether they are feelings of pain or joy, sadness or love, anger or intimacy.

The antidote to this sort of closed, controlling spirit is to learn to trust God with one's life. We can let go of the pains and disappointments of the past by allowing the living Christ to walk with us through difficult memories bringing healing and freedom. And we can offer up our uncertain futures to the care of the One who made us, knowing that God has promised to walk with us each step of the way. Perhaps such a walk will need the help of a wise counselor, pastor, or prayer partner. These steps need to be taken again and again until the process becomes a daily discipline in our lives. It is only when we can begin to open ourselves to the presence of God in our midst, at this very moment, that we can begin to be fully present to our children.

&

A story from Mark's gospel reveals how Jesus was fully present to the children in his midst.

> And they were bringing children to him, that he might touch them; and the disciples rebuked them. But when Jesus saw it he was indignant, and said to them, "Let the children come to me, do not hinder them; for to such belongs the kingdom of God. Truly, I say to you, whoever does not receive the kingdom of God like a child shall not enter it." And he took them in his arms and blessed them, laying his hands upon them.   —Mark 10:13-16

In reading the story, we must understand that there was no sentimentality about childhood in New Testament times. Children were valued because they would carry on the life and future of the people, but while they were still young they had no voice or rights. They were among the *anavim,* the little ones, the poor, outcast, and simple ones outside the mainstream of society.

When the disciples rebuked those bringing the children to Jesus, they were not being malicious. They were merely expressing the accepted view of the culture. Their rabbi was too important and influential to be wasting his time on children, or on women and Gentiles, for that matter (Luke 7:36-50, John 4:7-30).

Perhaps the parents of the children in the story understood the message of Jesus better than the disciples. They sensed something special about him. Yes, he was a powerful healer and many parents did bring their ailing children to be healed and set free at his hand, but these particular children were not sick. Their parents brought them solely to be in Jesus' presence. These parents intuitively knew that even though their little ones might not need physical healing and the subtleties of Jesus' teachings and stories would be lost on them, just being in his presence, being held in his arms, and looking into his smiling face would be a transforming experience for their children.

But the disciples felt otherwise. Their teacher and friend was at the height of his popularity. No doubt they were basking in the glory of it all. Just days before this incident with the children, Jesus had chided them for a discussion they had been having regarding who was the greatest among them.

> And he took a child, and put him in the midst of them; and taking him in his arms, he said to them, "Whoever receives one such child in my name receives me; and whoever receives me, receives not me but him who sent me." —Mark 9:36-37

Obviously the point did not sink in, for when these parents arrived with their children, the disciples were quick to send them away.

How often do we listen to the theory, and maybe even accept and espouse it, that we must value and protect our time with our children, and then turn right around and cut them off from our lives, our conversations, our worship? We all would love to be the patient parents carrying our little ones to Jesus, but how often are we not the proud and efficient disciples, protecting our master for more important things?

That attitude was intolerable to Jesus. The scripture says that he was "indignant." Some important principle was at stake here, and he was not willing to let it slide by. For he not only wanted to show his love and affection for these children by touching and blessing them, but he also knew that they had much to teach their elders. "For to such belongs the kingdom of God . . . . whoever does not receive the kingdom of God like a child shall not enter it."

Children can teach us to call God *Abba*, (Hebrew for "Daddy") with total abandon and total confidence in God's boundless love and power. Children can teach us to be simple and honest in our dealings. Children can teach us to live in the present with exhilaration and passion. Children can take us by the hand and lead us into the kingdom.

This simple and familiar story, so often depicted in flowery, idyllic landscapes, is important, not because it is sweet and touching, but because it turns everything upside down—our power structures, our ways of screening out the trivial from the significant, our ways of defining and controlling reality. Perhaps, just perhaps, it is vitally important for us to be spending meaningful time with our children, not because it is good for them, but because it is good for us.

&

Learning to be present to our children is a process that takes continual practice. It requires an attitude of the heart, a way of seeing, that embraces the incarnate presence of God in the midst of the ordinary and mundane.

As we think back to the happier memories of our own childhoods, is it only the impressive and well-orchestrated events that stick in our minds? Are not our hearts also warmed by the ordinary and spontaneous events that make up the life of a family—everyone cuddling in the big bed on Saturday morning, nibbling cookie dough in the kitchen, taking a ride in the country to feed the ducks, learning where the Big Dipper is for the first time. Such simple moments were not planned to be meaningful family times, but because of the open, spontaneous, and loving attitudes they encouraged, they are often more memorable and meaningful than the "this is going to be fun if it kills us" kind of outing that we can also recall. Often, such moments of joy and deep communication are not ones that we can control or create. But we can cultivate an attitude of awareness, a sensitivity to see that such moments are much more plentiful in our lives than we may realize.

Nathan had been born a month premature and caused us both a lot of stress and worry. He was a fussy baby, with lots of crying and spitting up. When he was about four months old, during one of those early-morning nursing times, Betsy had brought him into our bed in the hopes that maybe he would fall asleep afterwards, allowing her to catch a last snatch of sleep also. After nursing hungrily for a while, all of a sudden, he detached himself from her breast and looked up with a big grin, and they just spent the longest time gazing into each others' smiling faces. It was as if he was saying, "Hey, I get so busy fussing and eating that I forget it is you who's giving me this milk. And I love you." And Betsy seemed to be saying, "Sometimes I get so frazzled with diapers and spit-ups and housework that I forget what an amazing gift you are. I love you."

We can begin to see that these moments of recognition and loving communication can happen anywhere and that this attitude is adaptable to all those in-between times— waiting in lines at the grocery store, riding in the car, working in the kitchen, digging in the garden, washing the car, folding the laundry. A touch of the hand, a wink of the eye, a hug can communicate a tenderness deeper than words. A patient attitude of inviting the children to help, letting them into our world and its tasks can increase their sense of being connected with us and valued by us. A spontaneous game of alphabet in the car or a song made up as we travel can not only be a lot of fun, but can also let our children know that we value their company as much as we value listening to the news on the radio.

While it is important to cultivate attitudes of awareness and sensitivity in our ordinary routines, we should also realize that there will be times when we are to be totally available to our children and focused on active communication with them. There will be times when we need not only to include them in what we are doing, but also to put down what we are doing and spend some one-to-one time with them. Susanna Wesley, mother of ten, including John and Charles, found time to spend alone with each child during the week. Each one of our children needs to know how special it is for us to be alone with him or her. And often that means letting go of the idea that it ought to be a profoundly meaningful time. On a recent "alone time" with our daughter, John took her to the store to let her pick out a special snack and then they drove to a nearby state park, ate the snack, and had a discussion about Barbie dolls. It was her special time alone with him; he let her set the agenda.

But being able to fully say yes to our children, to give them our total attention, requires that we also learn to say no to them. This one is difficult for many of us. Those of us who are prone to feel guilty, perhaps because we are working outside of the home or because our children have special needs, tend to have difficulty saying no to our children's demands when we are physically near them.

Our son is deaf. He has a long bus ride to a special school. Communication with a world ignorant of sign language is difficult. Betsy has tended to want to compensate for these difficulties by being always available to him whenever he is around. A wise counselor who has been supporting our family through some difficult times has helped her to see that saying no to Nathan at the appropriate times is the most loving thing to do. He must learn that she is not just an extension of his own desires. He must be challenged to do for himself, to be with himself. It is a very obvious and simple truth, but one that had escaped her for a long time.

&

Did you ever wonder what ordinary everyday life with the growing boy Jesus was like for Mary and Joseph?

Certainly, he needed to be disciplined, potty-trained, and taught like any other child. Certainly, from time to time, Joseph and Mary must have had to remind one another of the holiness of the task entrusted to them. In Jesus' later teachings and parables, he had a wonderful knack for seeing marvelous insights into the kingdom in the most mundane things—yeast causing a loaf of bread to rise, a coin lost in the house, the sparrows, the wildflowers, salt, light, and seeds. Perhaps when he was still a toddler, Mary let him have his own little lump of dough as she kneaded and shaped the family loaves, or Joseph let him help scatter seed in the vegetable garden. It may be that as we invite our children into our day-to-day lives that these simple times of our being together will have a profound effect on them and us.

May each of us present-day parents have the humility and insight to see the living Christ in the everyday interactions with our precious children!

Three

Children of the Kingdom

WE HEAR A LOT THESE DAYS ABOUT FAMILY. We are inundated with information about everything from family restaurants to family worship services, family radio to family vacation spots. There seems to be a nostalgic longing for a time when families were stronger, more secure and predictable. An older friend recently was sharing that in spite of all the time-saving appliances and new opportunities for today's young families, she thinks that parents today are under much more stress than earlier generations because they are cut off from the rootedness of extended families. Thus the responsibility for holding the family together depends on the young family alone.

While there certainly is a great need to provide support and relief to over-stressed families, there is a subtle danger in making the ideal of "family" into an idol, the focus of all of one's thoughts and energies.

It is an attitude that can easily and dangerously creep into the church's self-understanding. The church's sole reason for being becomes to support and strengthen families and to promote traditional family values. The slogan "the family that prays together stays together" is typical of this misunderstanding. While the statement may be true, it seems to reflect distorted priorities. Do we pray and go to church to keep the status quo of our family together, or do we do so because there is a real and powerful God who wants to be present to, and transforming in, our lives and the lives of our families?

&

If our desire is to open ourselves to the real ministry and presence of Christ in our families, then perhaps we need to be willing to go where he has chosen to manifest his presence here on earth.

One of the amazing things about the church is that it is called the "Body of Christ." It is not said to be *like* the body of Christ or to *reflect* the body of Christ or to *point to* the body of Christ, but to *be* the body of Christ. Thus when the apostle Paul had been persecuting the fledgling church and he was confronted by the blinding presence of God on the road to Damascus, the voice from heaven said, "Saul, Saul, why do you persecute me?" (Acts 9:4) To persecute the followers of Jesus was to persecute Jesus himself, for he is present in his body. A family that wishes to grow spiritually and open itself to the powerful and healing presence of Christ *must* connect itself with the presence of that same Christ who dwells in the midst of his people, the church. When a family consciously seeks to be connected to the body of Christ, a whole new set of structures and allegiances are brought into the home.

Perhaps the most simple and powerful truth that a family can learn when it opens itself to involvement in the church is that it is a part of a living organism much broader and larger than itself and that *all* members of the family, both adults and children, are children of the kingdom and are under God's authority and care.

When parents worship together with their children they acknowledge that they are as needy and vulnerable as their little ones, that they do not know or understand everything, and that they are not in control of their lives and destinies. When individual families gather for worship with families that are different from themselves in race, income, ethnic background, or political outlook, they acknowledge that something more deep and profound than common interest draws them together. By being involved in this larger community they are living out the truth of their baptismal covenant, that by water and the Spirit they are born into God's family.

&

Jesus strongly affirmed the value and necessity of the family unit in his teaching and ministry. He affirmed the sanctity of marriage, railed against those who distorted religious obligations to avoid caring for their parents, and, frequently, in his stories and in his healing ministry, restored families to wholeness. One of his last concerns as he hung dying on the cross was to see that his mother would be cared for adequately.

Yet time and again, sometimes in very harsh and blunt words, Jesus radically subordinated the bond of kinship to the higher bond of fellowship within the kingdom of God.

> Then he went home; and the crowd came together again, so that they could not even eat. And when his family heard it, they went out to seize him, for people were saying, "He is beside himself."
>
> And his mother and his brothers came; and standing outside they sent to him and called him. And a crowd was sitting about him; and they said to him, "Your mother and your brothers are outside, asking for you." And he replied, "Who are my mother and my brothers?" And looking around on those who sat about him, he said, "Here are my mother and my brothers! Whoever does the will of God is my brother, and sister, and mother." —Mark 3:19-21,31-35

The incident took place near the beginning of Jesus' public ministry. He had just begun healing and teaching, and the reactions of the crowds were quite remarkable. They were following him everywhere, hanging on his every word, and pressing upon him to touch them and to heal their sick. Jesus himself was concerned for his own safety: "And he told his disciples to have a boat ready for him because of the crowd, lest they should crush him" (Mark 3:9).

Yet, in spite of his popularity, there was a strong current of opposition, especially among the religious leaders. They were concerned about his authority to forgive and to reinterpret the Sabbath laws, and some of them even felt that his miraculous powers came from demon possession.

It was a perfectly normal reaction for Jesus' family members to be concerned for his welfare. He and his new-found friends were so caught up in this movement that they did not even have the time or opportunity to eat. And the threats and accusations of the religious establishment were quite unsettling. Jesus' mother and brothers thought that it was their responsibility to intervene with Jesus, to encourage him to step back a little from his intense involvement and decide if he were really heading in the right direction.

Yet Jesus did not even stop what he was doing to address them directly. Rather, he seized the opportunity to teach his followers about the true nature of family loyalty. His bonding to those who do the will of God, who have left homes and security and careers to follow him ran much deeper than his bonding with his earthly family.

And although the Book of Acts records that his mother, Mary, and his brother, James, played important roles in the early church, it seems clear from the gospel accounts that this commitment of theirs came much later, and that there was a time when they were very ambivalent about their relationship with Jesus. Jesus did not nag or pressure them to be more fully involved in his earlier ministry. Neither did he feel that he had to defend and explain what he was doing to earn their approval and support. Rather, he was able to let go of the results and to move on in commitment with those who had become his kingdom family.

Jesus had his priorities straight and clear, and he demanded such singular devotion from his followers. His task was to proclaim the kingdom and to create a new family among those born into that kingdom. While he certainly welcomed his blood family into the kingdom, when they hesitated, he did not drop what he was doing to go patch things up with them.

His loyalty to his kingdom family was real and eternal. His sacrificial love for this new family was the foundation that allowed Jew and Greek, male and female, slave and free to be knit together in a new community that defied persecution and death and brought tremendous healing to individuals and family units as well.

&

A deep level of trust is established among those who share in a common faith. And a deep sense of humility is engendered in those who have made the decision to make Christ the center of their lives and their families each day. Though all the human vices of pettiness and power, hypocrisy and maliciousness have been present within the church, and will continue to be so until the Lord comes again, the church, by its very nature, is a place where we are meant to come without our competitive agenda, where we are meant to see what it means to be brothers and sisters made one through the gift of God's redemptive love. It is a place where we are meant to let our guard down, where we are not meant to spend our energies proving ourselves to be better or more important than someone else. Therefore, it is a place where we can seek wisdom and support in our individual and family struggles.

We have found it tremendously helpful over the years to have close spiritual friends, companions in the journey of faith who love us, listen to us, and speak the truth to us. At times, we can be going on and on, caught up in all the dilemmas of making important vocational decisions, caring for our family, and dealing with unfinished emotional business, when a few clear and loving words from a friend can cut through the fog and bring perspective again: "John, Betsy, are you praying? You know that when you do not pray, you fall apart."

Sometimes, as a couple, we get so caught up in our own conflicts and problems that we need to remember we are part of a larger community of faith, one that is available to help in our most vulnerable moments. Often just reaching out for help itself is healing.

&

Several years ago, we were living in an apartment in a busy part of town. Nathan, who was two-and-a-half years old at the time, had gotten out of our tiny yard when Betsy was not paying attention and had wandered into a busy intersection, his deafness rendering him totally oblivious to the screeching brakes and honking horns. We found him across the street at the grocery store where someone had taken him. Thank God he survived the incident unharmed.

Betsy was devastated by the experience, yet within several weeks she failed once more to close the gate, and it nearly happened again! Fortunately, someone had grabbed Nathan at the curb as he was about to bound across the busy intersection.

As we talked about the incident that evening, sparks began to fly. Betsy was very sorry but fully aware that being sorry was not enough. Nathan could very well be dead, and being sorry would not bring him back. John was desperate. What could be done to protect their child? He could not just say, "Oh, that's okay dear, just don't let it happen again," because it *had* happened again, and the next time we might not be so fortunate.

We were at a stalemate, both aware that something had to be done, both too upset to know how to proceed. So we called Bill and Sue, two of our close Christian friends, briefly explained the situation, asked for prayers, and hung up the phone. We did not expect to receive any sympathy or advice, we just wanted the knowledge that someone outside of our web of hurt and confusion was lifting us up into God's grace.

Immediately the atmosphere in the room changed. We knew we were no longer hopelessly alone, and a whole new quality entered our discussion.

Instead of just feeling bad about the careless gatekeeping, Betsy was able to realize and express a need to use more common sense, and began to pray daily that God would bring to her mind the ordinary and practical needs of the family. John, on the other hand, began to see a larger picture, one that included the need for us to find a safer environment for our children, and he was challenged to begin a search for a safe, affordable home for the family. Because we had reached out for help, we were able to challenge and support, rather than attack, each other in these new ventures.

One wonderful advantage to being involved in the life of the church as a family is that we learn that we can reach out for such help to our own family members. The rigid roles of parent and child can break down as we discover our common need to seek God's grace together as children of the kingdom. It is often the younger ones who lead their parents into deeper faithfulness.

Betsy vividly remembers one frazzled day when her temper was getting shorter and shorter. She finally came to her senses and realized that she was being unreasonable. She stopped and asked our little daughter to forgive her for her bad attitude and to pray for her. Shemaleiah did forgive her, and, laying hands on her, prayed a simple prayer to ask God to help her mother. And that prayer was answered.

Several days later, when the fatigue and grumpiness had set in again, Shemaleiah came up to her mother and sweetly said, "Mommy, I think I need to pray for you." Betsy was cut to the quick and humbly grateful for her daughter's ministry to her. Both mother and daughter were both learning the marvelous mystery of the kingdom, that being sisters in the journey of faith takes precedence over the traditional role differences suggested by age.

Finding one's allegiance with those who are doing the will of God, joining the journey of faith with one's fellow believers, goes much deeper than merely showing up at a church on Sunday mornings. But public, communal worship as a family is a very important aspect of spiritual health.

Church communities have developed many different arrangements for meeting the worship and educational needs of their families. Finding the right balance between child-centered time, adult-centered time, and family-centered time is often very difficult. Each community and family must struggle with their local possibilities and find a mix that works for them, knowing that all arrangements can be modified. Some communities encourage the children to worship with the adults fully and frequently, and they are able to adjust to the happy chaos that ensues. Others prefer to have a separate children's worship service with the whole community coming together only occasionally.

While we love to affirm to our children that they are members of the Body of Christ and are always welcome at the altar of the Lord, there are times when we walk out of church feeling like we have barely survived World War III. At times like those, it is a great relief to know that creative and meaningful children's programs are available to allow us the opportunity to worship quietly and calmly. It is important to allow children to be children and adults to be adults, remembering that we are all together vital members of the Body of Christ.

Developing a sense of humor is invaluable as we seek to be more and more involved in the church. Sometimes our families get so serious about being religious that we end up walking away in disappointment when the church at the corner does not live up to our high expectations. We are quick to judge the foibles of others and quick to turn away without realizing that we are all in this together. Someone whose name is lost to us, but whose wisdom is not, once said, "The church is a hospital for sinners, not a museum for saints." That person was right, we think. If we keep waiting for the perfect church, we will lose precious opportunities for our own imperfections to be refined.

Somehow, it always seems that chaos descends on our household on Sunday morning. "Where are my shoes?" "Why didn't you wash my good pants?" "Why are we always running late no matter how early we get up?" "Would you two quit throwing books at each other in the back seat?" And we wonder, as we walk down the aisle frazzled and tense, whether we really belong here, whether we deserve to talk to God after talking to our children the way we did in the car. And then, down on our knees, after a deep breath, we know that, of course, we never deserve to be in God's presence, but that this is where we desperately need to be, alongside all the other fallible human beings who have fallen short of God's best and are willing to admit it. Somehow, in the midst of our inadequate church structures and our inadequate families, God is present with us and that changes everything.

&

Imagine how Mary and Joseph felt raising their special child in the religious establishment of their day. Perhaps they questioned whether the corner synagogue in Nazareth and the ordinary rabbi in charge were adequate to the task of educating their son.

The scriptures tell us that when Jesus was twelve years old he travelled with his parents to Jerusalem for the Passover Festival. Do you think their household was perfectly calm as they prepared for the big trip, packing up the best sandals, the best robes, and the right food for the journey? Certainly the trip home was nothing close to calm. Jesus had disappeared totally. Perhaps Mary and Joseph, hot and tired, were blaming each other, "But I thought you said your uncle Jacob was looking after him?" "Didn't you even check where he was when we stopped for water at the last well?" And when they found him in the Temple after three days of searching, his response may have seemed very unsatisfactory to them: "How is it that you sought me? Did you not know that I must be in my Father's house?" (Luke 2:49) Joseph and Mary, perhaps puzzled and uncertain, took him home to Nazareth. They were beginning to learn that the family to which he was called was much larger than their own and that they must learn to let go of him.

May our own participation in the church community, as puzzling and frustrating as it can be at times, remind us that along with our children, we are all part of a body of believers, a larger family, that transcends time and space and history.

Four

The Battle of the Bathtub

AS PARENTS, WE EXERCISE AUTHORITY over our children. We choose where they will be born, what language they will be taught, what name will identify them for the rest of their lives, and into which religious community they will be initiated. Our choices and assumptions, for good or ill, will be with our children for a lifetime. The issue is not whether we will have authority in our children's lives, but how we will view that authority and how we will use it.

We find that our authority as parents is most satisfying and easily embraced when it is rooted in service. This model of servant authority is demonstrated in the life of Jesus.

As we reflect upon him, we see that he was a strong and powerful figure. His word healed the sick, cast out unclean spirits, quieted the storm and the waves. He spoke boldly to kings and religious authorities. Yet how did he show authority in the lives of his followers? By loving service—by speaking a compassionate word of forgiveness to a condemned adulteress, by washing the feet of his friends, by patiently explaining his message to thick-headed disciples, by cooking breakfast on the seashore, by taking time to respond to the needs of a frightened woman in the crowd.

Jesus was a servant, and that role, which found perfect fulfillment at the cross, was one he freely chose. And because he freely chose it, he was neither a slave nor a doormat. When one freely chooses to be a servant, a confidence and a boldness comes that is rarely present in one unwillingly forced to be a slave. In the multifaceted ways in which we are daily called to be an authority in the lives of our children, we can, along with Christ, freely choose to serve them. And as we do so, we can learn a new simplicity and freedom.

&

During one of the busiest times in Jesus' ministry, he and his disciples headed into Gentile territory for a little rest and relaxation, to get away from the demands of the needy crowds. Soon, however, their solitude was broken.

> And behold, a Canaanite woman from that region came out and cried, "Have mercy on me, O Lord, Son of David; my daughter is severely possessed by a demon." But he did not answer her a word. And his disciples came and begged him, saying, "Send her away, for she is crying after us." He answered, "I was sent only to the lost sheep of the

house of Israel." But she came and knelt before him, saying, "Lord, help me." And he answered, "It is not fair to take the children's bread and throw it to the dogs." She said, "Yes, Lord, yet even the dogs eat the crumbs that fall from their masters' table." Then Jesus answered her, "O woman, great is your faith! Be it done for you as you desire." And her daughter was healed instantly.

—Matthew 15:22-28

The harshness of this story often closes our ears to what it has to teach us as parents. Jesus was in fact being consistent with his mission, which was to the Jews. It was the task of his followers to carry that message to the Gentile world. The distinction is between his earthly mission to the Jews and his willingness to respond to faith wherever it was found. And this amazing woman would not let him go without a response! She knew that she had authority to care for the spiritual and physical health of her child, and she was bold and confident in acting upon that authority, but she also had the humility to know from whence that authority was ultimately derived.

Mark's gospel states that she left her ailing child at home and ventured out on her own to find Jesus. For a woman to be travelling alone, and for a Gentile woman to be initiating a conversation with a Jewish man, took a lot of nerve. Her love for, and willingness to serve, her suffering daughter, was profound. She was desperate for help, and she must have grasped onto the stories of Jesus that were trickling over the border from Israel, particularly the ones about his miraculous healings. In her hope and desperation, she risked taking action. She packed up and went out looking for Jesus.

How disappointing it must have been when her request seemed to fall on deaf ears, when the disciples began shooing her away, and Jesus spoke not a word. And when he finally did speak, it was only to say that he had not come to help people like her. One with less courage and less tenacity would have been devastated by his remarks. But this woman, with a clear sense of her child's need and her desire to see that need met, was not fazed by his off-putting remarks. She simply and straightforwardly got down on her knees before him and said, "Lord, help me." And when he put her off again—"It is not fair to take the children's bread and throw it to the dogs"—she came right back again, "Yes, Lord, yet even the dogs eat the crumbs that fall from their masters' table."

Usually when Jesus spoke in symbols or parables, everyone, and especially the disciples, became confused: "Huh? What are you talking about? What does it all mean?" Not only did this woman understand, but she entered right in and spoke back to *him* in a parable! This is the only example recorded in the Gospels of such a thing ever happening, and Jesus, amazed and touched by the depth of her understanding and faith and surely moved by the depth of her love and commitment to her daughter, healed the child from afar.

This woman served her child by doing what her child was not able to do on her own. She took great risks to go to God on behalf of her child, even to the point of receiving personal insult and rejection. In the face of that rejection, she would not take no for an answer. She continued to defend the needs of her child, while always affirming that both she and her daughter were dependent on God for any healing or wholeness. She demonstrated true humility. She knew that she and her daughter were valuable, deserving of Jesus' love, attention, and effort, yet she recognized that any attention or healing Jesus might give was pure gift.

&

How do we use the gift of parental authority wisely? We are not often faced with the same life and death situation as the desperate mother who sought out Jesus' help in the story. But we are all faced with the challenge to set the standards and determine the directions in our homes. How do we make the daily decisions that deeply affect the atmosphere of our homes? Who sets the tone at the dinner table? Who gets to use the car? How late can the children stay up or out? How is a whiny attitude dealt with? How is TV and VCR use monitored, or is it? Who does what chores and when?

When we can begin to see that we are to use our authority to *serve* and that, indeed, it is in serving that we participate most fully with the ministry that Christ has to our children, then we can develop principles by which to make such everyday, mundane decisions.

The way Christ serves and relates within each individual home, and how he calls each of us to participate with him, will be very different. There are no easy and clear-cut rules, but when we are willing to grow and willing to believe that we are not alone, our journey becomes more hopeful.

&

Some of us may have great difficulty in taking strong, clear actions of authority with our children. Our style may be to "hang loose," as we find it easier to do things ourselves or bend the rules a little rather than to force confrontations. We can easily be talked into providing alternative meals should our children not like what is served, or into stretching the bedtime or extending the deadlines for tasks to be done. When we truly open ourselves to serve our children with the authority that Christ gives, we may find that we are being gently prodded into new and difficult behaviors.

Our son was having great difficulties in school because of resistive behavior. With the help and support of the Christian community and the school community, we were encouraged to take specific steps to help Nathan choose to be more cooperative. The kind of confrontive discipline that was part of the new plan was very uncomfortable for Betsy and her relaxed parenting style. Betsy would often fluctuate between feeling sorry for Nathan having to deal with so many demands and feeling sorry for herself at having to put up with such a difficult child. A significant turning point came one evening during "the battle of the bathtub."

John was working that night, our daughter was quietly doing her homework, and Nate definitely needed a bath. He was very resistive to this idea, so Betsy did as she was instructed to do, to only make demands that she was willing to follow through on and to make Nathan uncomfortable until he was willing to comply. Betsy held his arms up until he would choose to take his bath. Her mind immediately began a game of "Poor Nate, maybe if I bend a little and let him watch TV first he will come around later" and quickly proceeded to a round of "Poor Betsy, why does this always happen when John isn't around to help, and what about all the work that I need to get done while I'm stuck here locked in a battle of wills with this stubborn kid?"

Often Nathan would give in before her mind had worked through its little set of pitying games. But this particular evening, he was quite determined *not* to set foot near the bathtub. Betsy had nearly reached the end of her rope when she recalled a prayer time that she and Nate had with a Christian friend earlier in the day. In the quiet that morning, she had very strongly felt the presence of Christ showing her that the program of discipline we were undertaking was truly good for Nathan, and that as we served Nate by helping him to control his own actions and responses, Christ himself was with us serving Nate.

As God's grace opened her to recall that truth, she was able to see this difficult confrontation not as something that she must simply try to endure because she was told she should do it, but as ministry with Christ to Nathan. It was amazing how quickly her attitude was transformed! She was still physically exhausted, but when Nate finally decided to give in, she was able to move on from the experience without anger or resentment and has been able to follow through since then with much greater ease and peace.

Others of us may have a very firm and strict parenting style. We may tend to overcontrol and make harsh demands on our children, not because that is necessarily the best for *them*, but because it is easier for *us*. Such an atmosphere is described in a verse of John's song *More Rain Tomorrow*.

> Alice sits alone now with her family.
> No one cares to understand
> the way she'd like to be.
> They only want her to be like them.

We may need to open our hearts to hear Christ's servant authority calling us to listen more intently to the needs of our child's heart. We may need to be willing to negotiate and change, to take the extra time, energy, and patience required to let our child try something new, turning over to him or her some of the responsibility we have been holding on to.

It may be that we have already discovered a fairly balanced and comfortable parenting style. To consciously and willingly acknowledge that Christ is present with us in the little day-to-day ways that we work with our children can strengthen us and prepare us for the new challenges that are always arising.

Our confidence and humility grow when we consistently choose to unite our efforts with the serving nature of Christ, when we realize the source of our authority. And because the presence of Christ within our relationship with our children is a lively and active spirit, it can carry us and teach us to be servants in the diverse needs and situations that we face. To serve as with Christ's loving authority would be very different for a parent dealing with a seven-year-old's inability to keep a bedroom clean from that of a parent dealing with a sixteen-year-old's abuse of alcohol. Jesus himself dealt differently with the rich young ruler (Luke 18:18-30) and the woman caught in adultery (John 8:1-11). Jesus' firm compassion longs to be made flesh in each situation we may face with our children. His strong presence can make clear in our hearts the answer to the question: How can I best serve my child in this setting?

The fruit of our struggles to serve our children with Christlike authority is that the children themselves will experience what godly service is like. They can come to know respect and humility by responding to the firm and loving direction we give. They can learn that their primary goal in this life is not to seek to have their own needs met, but rather to reach out in service to others.

&

The scriptures tell us that after that difficult and mysterious incident in the Temple when Jesus was twelve years old, he went home to Nazareth with his parents "and was obedient to them" (Luke 2:51). Another passage states that "he learned obedience" (Hebrews 5:8). Could it have been difficult for Mary and Joseph to discipline their son, especially living with the knowledge that he was somehow very special?

We can imagine that the skilled carpenter, Joseph, must have exercised patience and restraint when he taught the craft to his adopted son, allowing Jesus to help him on tasks that would have been easier for him to have completed himself, demanding that he learn to care for and put away the tools properly, teaching him to serve and respect the fellow villager who had requested a yoke to be fashioned for his oxen or a table to be created for his home, insisting that Jesus work carefully and lovingly.

We can imagine that Mary included him in her household tasks, and by expecting him to be faithful in feeding the animals, filling the lamps, and tidying the house, she taught him the value of serving. Perhaps Jesus needed to be reminded to keep his room clean. Perhaps he had trouble grasping the intricacies of Hebrew grammar at the synagogue school and needed the extra push of Joseph encouraging him in his homework.

Whatever those unchronicled years were filled with, we know that Jesus learned well how to offer loving and disciplined service. He knew how to unself-consciously wrap a towel around his waist and wash the feet of those wearied by a day of travel. He knew how to build a fire and cook a meal. He knew how to answer patiently the questions of those who were puzzled by the images and stories in his teachings. He knew the simplicity and the authority of servanthood because he had been under the authority of those who loved and served him well.

The authority we exercise in our children's lives is a great responsibility. May we seek God's help and guidance as we use that authority wisely to serve the ones entrusted to our care.

Five

Extravagant Forgiveness

THERE IS SOMETHING RECKLESS AND EXTRAVAGANT about forgiving. To bear a grief, a hurt, or an insult, to feel the pain and then choose to let go of that hurt and receive the offender back into one's heart is a risky and unsettling thing.

Jesus once told the story of a father with such an extravagant love, a father who welcomed his "prodigal son" home from a life of irresponsible pleasure seeking. When the older brother, the one who stayed home and worked hard, saw the joyful reunion, he was incensed at the unfairness of it. And he was right, it was not fair. Says Lewis Smedes in

Forgive and Forget, "Forgiveness seems almost unnatural. Our sense of fairness tells us people should pay for the wrong they do. But forgiving is love's power to break nature's rule."

True forgiveness can only come from the overflow of an abundantly loving and compassionate heart. Such mercy does not come naturally to most of us. It is itself a gracious gift that must be sought, received, and cultivated. For without the ability to forgive, the human heart grows cold and dies. Whereas forgiveness flows out of love, unforgiveness flows out of pride, a harsh self-centeredness that refuses to see one's own connectedness to the human condition and the faults of others. And each self-centered resolve that is intended to punish the offending party—"I'll never forgive him for what he said," "I'll never speak to her again"—only builds more walls that push others away and keep love out.

Wise counselors and doctors have always known that there is a unity of body and spirit, so that holding in anger, resentments, and grudges does damage to one's body as well as one's soul. And although Jesus refused to make a one-to-one correlation between sin and illness, he made it clear that in the process of making a person whole the forgiveness of sins was just as essential as the mending of limbs. Thus he could say to the paralytic lowered through the roof by his friends, "My son, your sins are forgiven. I say to you, rise, take up your pallet and go home" (Mark 2:5,11). We are wise to cultivate hearts that are willing to forgive for the sake of healing and personal wholeness, as well as for the sake of restoring broken relationships.

A husband has not forgiven his wife for bouncing a check. He comes home and yells at the kids who had nothing to do with the bad check. A forty-year-old man continues to have infrequent and negative interchanges with his father because he has never quite recovered from the divorce that his parents went through thirty years before. Two elderly and widowed sisters who live in the same town refuse to communicate because of a slight that took place decades ago at the elder sister's wedding reception. A mother with a handicapped child continues to grieve over the loss of her child's sight and to blame herself for a difficulty in the birth; her sadness is reflected in her child, the child who says that she wishes she could die and go to heaven where she would be able to see.

The old adage that time heals all hurts is not always true. In fact, it may be more difficult to deal with past hurts because we feel foolish that such old experiences should still have a hold on us.

If we as parents want to model an open, generous, and forgiving spirit in our homes, we must be willing to look at areas of our lives where we have blocked that spirit. Often our present problems flow from unhealthy dynamics established when we were children. If we are to grow, we need to reflect back upon our lives, taking responsibility for our part in the imperfections of our families and forgiving those who have hurt us. Our willingness to go back to difficult memories, to detach the offending person from the hurt and to let go of the pain, is a spiritual surgery that can transform our way of viewing that person, even if he or she is long dead. It is not an easy process and will usually take time.

We can suggest some ways that might help in approaching this whole area of dealing with past hurts. You could go to a retreat center and meet with a spiritual director or counselor who could lead you toward a forgiving spirit through silence and prayer or perhaps writing about past hurts. If a retreat is not possible, you could set aside fifteen minutes a day for quiet time, asking God to help you identify and resolve past hurts and places of unforgiveness. You may find that talking with a trusted friend, a spouse, or a counselor can spur new awareness. If the abuse of alcohol, food, or drugs has been part of your personal or family life, twelve-step groups such as Alcoholics Anonymous, Al-Anon, Narcotics Anonymous, Overeaters Anonymous, and Adult Children of Alcoholics can be very supportive in helping you come to terms with the hurts and resentments of the past and move ahead to new behaviors and patterns. A combination of any of these approaches may also be appropriate to your particular needs and situation.

After discovering the hurts, you will be ready to begin the hard work of reconciliation. You may choose to meet with or write to those persons from whom you have been estranged. Sometimes in a relationship there may be just a little hurt, like an irritating splinter. You may feel the problem is so small that it is not worth the effort of talking about it, or you may feel silly or petty in bringing it up. Yet you will know if the splinter is affecting the relationship. Have courage not only with big problems but also with splinters.

There is no place where these demons of the past become so evident as when we begin to raise our own children. Unresolved hatred and bitterness is like a cancer in the soul. Hatred, resentment, or bitterness brings darkness to our souls; love cannot flourish until they are removed. When we offer forgiveness to others, they may not accept our forgiveness. Jesus was asked by a disciple, "How many times should I forgive my brother?" In essence, Jesus replied, "You should always forgive your brother. There is no limit to the amount of times forgiveness should be offered."

For us to benefit from a forgiving spirit, we need to keep forgiving, even when our attempts at reconciliation are rejected. It is easy to become angry and hurt if these attempts are rebuffed or ignored. A forgiving spirit needs the grace of God to sustain its courage.

&

In letting go of the excess baggage from the past, we first need to forgive ourselves. If we are the kind of people who walk around with negative thoughts filling our heads, reminding ourselves of the ways we fall short, perhaps we need to apply the same principles of forgiveness to ourselves that we would to others. In summarizing the heart of the law, Jesus said that we must love God with all of our heart, soul, mind, and strength and that we must love our neighbor as ourselves (Mark 12:29-31). Certainly, we will be unable to forgive and love others unless we learn to forgive and love ourselves. We may need some gentle surgery of the soul in order to detach ourselves from the wrongs we have committed in the past, to let go of them and move ahead. We can often most successfully do this in the presence of caring counselors or clergy.

As we seek to teach our children a loving and forgiving attitude in our home by modelling it in our own lives, we are called back again and again to the source of all-forgiving love. Nowhere is the powerful and radical love of God more clearly demonstrated than at the cross, where Jesus— betrayed by a friend, forsaken by those who loved him, maligned by the religious establishment, and tormented and crucified by the government troops—looks down from that cross and says, "Father, forgive them, for they know not what they do" (Luke 23:34). Here at the cross of Jesus we see in love's eyes a place to bring all the unhealed hurts, the stubborn and bitter resentments that refuse to go away, the cold walls of pride that keep us from mending the brokenness of the past, the self-justifying cries of "It's not fair!" Here at the cross of Jesus we have the opportunity to let go of all the self-condemnation and to let Christ's radical forgiveness soften and transform our hearts.

In our own lives, coming to the cross is a daily process to let that transformation take place. It is a gift, not something we can create by a certain formula. But we can make ourselves available to receive that gift.

When we begin our days with prayer, looking out onto our country backyard, our minds are often filled with recriminations for all the things that we did not accomplish the day before, or self-pitying thoughts about all the help and appreciation we feel we deserve but are not receiving. Before we launch into formal morning prayers, we spend a few minutes in quiet. Sometimes we are so entrenched in our own negativity that we refuse to listen, and walk off into the day carrying our burdens.

But more often than not, as we allow the quiet of God's presence in, there is an opportunity to let go. Sometimes it is the morning star still ablaze, or the rose-colored clouds at dawn, or the sight of a squirrel scurrying that reminds us of the presence and reality of One so much greater than our pettiness and worries, who took on our burdens at the cross and gave back love. Here we learn that love begets love, forgiving begets forgiving, and that this spirit that is discovered at the cross can be carried into our day, and can be discovered by our children.

&

Jesus taught much about forgiveness as well as demonstrating its power at the cross.

> Therefore the kingdom of heaven may be compared to a king who wished to settle accounts with his servants.

When he began the reckoning, one was brought to him who owed him ten thousand talents; and as he could not pay, his lord ordered him to be sold, with his wife and children and all that he had, and payment to be made. So the servant fell on his knees, imploring him, "Lord, have patience with me, and I will pay you everything." And out of pity for him the lord of that servant released him and forgave him the debt. But that same servant, as he went out, came upon one of his fellow servants who owed him a hundred denarii; and seizing him by the throat he said, "Pay what you owe." So his fellow servant fell down and besought him, "Have patience with me, and I will pay you." He refused and went and put him in prison till he should pay the debt. When his fellow servants saw what had taken place, they were greatly distressed, and they went and reported to their lord all that had taken place. Then his lord summoned him and said to him, "You wicked servant! I forgave you all that debt because you besought me; and should not you have had mercy on your fellow servant, as I had mercy on you?" And in anger his lord delivered him to the jailers, till he should pay all his debt. So also my heavenly Father will do to every one of you, if you do not forgive your brother from your heart.

—Matthew 18:23-35

Forgiveness, if truly received, enlarges the heart and begets more forgiveness. This is a truth that Jesus took very seriously indeed; this parable about forgiveness is one of the sternest passages in the Gospels.

The king was most likely an oriental despot, and his servant was a high officer of the state who had defaulted on payment of revenue. Ten thousand talents was an incredibly large sum of money, something that would take decades of labor to pay back. On the other hand, one hundred *denarii* was a manageable debt, the wages of a day's work. In his parables, Jesus often used hyperbole to make the point.

What is emphasized here is the incredible difference in the two debts owed and the absolute absurdity of the man who, after being forgiven a crushing lifelong debt, would not have mercy on his fellow servant whose debt was minor.

The forgiveness that God poured out for us at the cross knows no measure. Likewise, our own forgiveness should be generous as we reach out to those who have done us wrong. If we cut ourselves off from others through the hardness of our hearts, we will find that we are cutting ourselves off from God.

How do we let the power of God's forgiving love into our families? How do we cultivate the generosity of spirit that does not keep an account of all the wrongs and injustices it has suffered?

We do it imperfectly, in bits and pieces. We do it, not as experts lecturing our children, but as fellow travellers, struggling alongside them in a broken world where we too often feel the sting of unfairness. If we are to teach our children to take responsibility for their actions and attitudes, we should first take responsibility for our own behaviors, opening ourselves to the searching light of the Holy Spirit. Lest we feel overwhelmed, let us remember that the power of God's forgiving love is always being given and is already present and at work in our families.

We are able to forgive when we know that we are forgiven. We are able to love when we know that we are loved. In Christ, God has both forgiven and loved us completely—body, soul, mind, and spirit—to the deepest level of our being. Through grace, we are already equipped to live in a godly way. And this power has been given to parents and children alike.

God's abundant love and forgiveness is the hope, the absolute assurance that is the foundation for building reconciled relationships in a Christian family. On this basis, we can trust that God's loving and forgiving spirit is available to our families.

&

Each family can discover and participate in God's abundant love and forgiveness in its own way. We have found some ways that work in our family. As a couple, we try to keep our relationship as open and up-to-date as possible, not letting annoyances or resentments fester. Though there are times when we forget or intentionally ignore the injunction, we try to be faithful to Paul's wise advice not to let the sun go down on our anger (Ephesians 4:26). Sometimes that means some very late nights spent hashing things out, but it has been a worthwhile habit to cultivate. When we are loving and forgiving to one another, that spirit spreads to the children. When we are in the midst of some conflict or unresolved issue between us, we do our best not to belittle one another by trying to get the children on our side of an issue. We help each other to become aware of childhood patterns we have unquestioningly adopted and encourage one another to grow beyond them. We have found that generosity of spirit can be cultivated in little things. So can forgiveness. Indeed, it is often in the little things that we have the greatest opportunities for growth.

Betsy grew up in a large and not particularly wealthy family. Special treats such as sodas, candy, and ice cream bars were rationed. They were something that were cherished, hoarded, or bargained with, but rarely just given away freely. On the other hand, John grew up in the wealthy home of a candy executive. Treats were always on hand and freely shared with children in the neighborhood. It has taken Betsy many years of gentle reminders to herself not to act like an eight-year-old protecting her stash when she is given a special treat and instinctively does not want to share it. She has had to learn to appreciate the little treasures of her childhood without reverting to the stinginess.

We heard a story about a woman who had purchased colorful, new upholstery for the window seat in her dining room. When a family member inadvertently burned a hole in the new cushion, she was certainly disappointed. But she forgave the mishap and used her needlework skills to cover the hole with a lovely flower. Now, instead of looking at the ugly hole and feeling the sting of disappointment, she can see the flower and remember the creative and transforming power of love.

Sometimes though, even in the little things, forgiveness does not flow so easily. We remember being newlyweds, busy writing thank-you notes for wedding presents. Betsy ran out of stamps and wanted to get the notes in the mail, so when Betsy found some of John's stamps, she used them. They were a bit outdated, so she had to match them up with some one-cent stamps, but at least the letters got in the mail. Little did she realize that these were a very special one-of-a-kind issue of stamps because they had printing on the back. John had purchased them years earlier, knowing that they would become quite valuable due to their uniqueness. Later, when he discovered what Betsy had done, he was furious. He could not believe she had done such a foolish thing and would not let her hear the end of it. Betsy was genuinely sorry for her mistake and even offered to try to track down the notes and get the stamps back, even though they would have been cancelled. John refused her offer and said that he forgave her, but for months he would continue to bring up the incident, reminding her of her great offense.

Finally, we sat down and discussed the whole thing. Betsy challenged the reality of his forgiveness: "Don't forgive me if you don't want to, but if you have forgiven me, then quit bringing the issue up." John relented and agreed that he would never again bring up the stamps unless Betsy initiated the conversation. The forgiveness was finally real. Now the stamp fiasco is a funny memory we share. Learning to challenge and support one another in the little ways of fostering a generous and forgiving spirit can create the climate for bigger steps of growth.

&

Bob and Susan had a close-knit, stable family. Their children were eleven and six, and they got along quite well. A loving atmosphere filled the home. But the oldest child, a girl, often seemed quite depressed and despondent for no apparent reason. On the other hand, their son was lively and cheerful.

After reflecting together upon the differences in their children's attitudes, Bob and Susan decided to pray together for their daughter after she was asleep. As they stood near her bed that night and opened themselves to how God would have them pray, Susan was suddenly led back in her mind to the time of her pregnancy. Their first child had been conceived much sooner than either parent had planned. They were still newlyweds with schooling to complete. The financial situation was very unsettling. In particular, Susan felt invaded by this new life that was thrust upon her.

As they prayed, she was startled by the intensity of those long-forgotten feelings. Once her daughter was born, she had coped well as a mother. She had loved and accepted her daughter. She had forgotten the strong feelings of resentment that had so pervaded her pregnancy. In the quiet of that prayer time, and in the presence of her husband and her sleeping daughter, she asked God to forgive her for the anger and resentment that she had felt toward her daughter so long ago, and together Bob and Susan prayed for God to heal their daughter of any hurt that may have resulted from those feelings. The next morning, their daughter came bounding down the stairs and jumped joyfully onto her parents' bed. It had been the first time in her life that she had done that. In a mysterious way, she had been set free by the power of forgiving love. Only the searchlight of the Spirit of God can bring to our minds such deep and powerful surgery of the heart.

Few families today are untouched by the brokenness of our needy world. How great are our opportunities to forgive and be forgiven, and thus to be a part of God's transforming work.

&

We can only wonder what hardships Mary suffered in her small-town community when it became evident that she was pregnant before her wedding day.

Certainly, it must have been very painful when she heard that her beloved had resolved to break off their engagement. An angelic visitor changed Joseph's mind, but who dealt with the sting in her heart, the sadness at not being trusted?

What sort of ridicule may Joseph have endured from his companions? Perhaps they laughed that the quiet and faithful Joseph could not restrain his passions, or else they thought him the fool for wedding a woman spoiled by someone else. Imagine how it felt to give birth to your child in a stable and to be forced to flee into the night soon after to escape Herod's sword. Certainly, being refugees in the strange land of Egypt must have been difficult for a new family.

The scriptures do not tell of those inner struggles. But certainly there would have been plenty of reason for a young couple to feel embittered and resentful. Yet their child grew strong and was filled with a spirit of compassion that reached out to those who most desperately needed to know that they were forgiven. Perhaps he learned at his parents' knees how the power to forgive could transform even the most bitter village gossip, and how the healed memory could see a difficult and lonely journey as a time of gracious provision.

Mary and Joseph, along with their child, made the risky and unsettling choice to forgive. May our hearts be enlarged to journey with them.

Six

Healing in the Family

NOTHING CHALLENGES OUR FAITH AND TRUST in God's goodness more than when we see those we love suffer. To actively reach out for healing in such difficult times is to risk believing that God's mercy is abundant, that indeed, God is a good god who desires wholeness for his children.

Getting involved with healing is a risky business. It opens us to disappointments and failure. It calls us to honesty about our deepest desires, fears, and vulnerabilities. It challenges us to step out into the darkness in faith and trust that God will be there to meet us. It causes us to ask the most basic and fundamental question—is God's power real in my life or not?

Because of the risks, many believers have simply avoided the whole issue of spiritual healing. The stories of a few charlatans, along with a theology that relegates "all those miracles" either to Bible times or to the pious imaginations of Bible writers, keep those who are uncertain safely distant from the idea of healing. Others may feel that only particularly saintly people could ever hope to see such a powerful manifestation of God's presence. For the vast majority of us, spiritual healing has just not been a part of our common reality, and the fear of the unknown and the fear of failure keep us from entering this part of Christ's ministry. Yet as we read through the pages of scripture, especially the Gospels, we are invited again and again to let go of our preconceptions and to embrace this Jesus who very much walked among us as a healer.

&

Jesus touched such a great variety of people with his healing presence—from social outcasts to religious authorities, from aggressive beggars to meek and self-effacing bystanders hiding in the crowds, from young children to ailing mothers-in-law. He touched the humble and desperate, the proud and self-pitying, those appreciative of his work and those who walked away without a word of thanks. He touched very ordinary people who came to him with their doubts and struggles, their longings and fears. He accepted and loved them right where they were, and he called them to fullness of life.

In Jesus' ministry, healing was not restricted to alleviating physical symptoms. His message of salvation was a message of wholeness for both body and soul. Wholeness included a healed self-image as much as the mending of a withered arm, the reconciliation of a family as much as the opening of blind eyes, the forgiveness of sins as much as the cleansing of a dreaded disease. The woman who had suffered hemorrhaging for twelve years—and had thus been cut off from her husband and the faith community because she was ritually unclean—came to Jesus for physical healing, hiding in the crowd, hoping to touch the fringe of his garment without being noticed. But though Jesus' power did heal her, Jesus did not let her go until he could look into her eyes and speak words of encouragement to her soul: "Daughter, your faith has made you well; go in peace" (Luke 8:48).

As well as recognizing the unity between body and soul, Jesus also recognized the importance of community. When he healed an individual, he restored that person to the community. Thus he told the cleansed lepers to go show themselves to the priest and offer the proper sacrifices that would bring them back into the mainstream of their communities. Often it was in the context of restoring wholeness to the family that Jesus' ministry of healing took place. He rebuked the fever of Peter's mother-in-law, and she immediately got on her feet and began serving her extended family. He saw the plight of the young widow of Nain, left without a husband and now bereft of her son, and he raised the boy to life so the family unit could continue.

How do we, ordinary twentieth-century Christians, come to know the healing and reconciling work of Christ within our bodies and souls, within our families and communities? How do we affirm the healing power of God in the world, when all around us and deep within us we see and sense so much brokenness and alienation? How do we find courage to get involved in the risky business of healing?

Our first step is the step of faith—faith that God is good and that God cares. It seems very simple and obvious, but often it is the most difficult step to take. Often in times of pain or crisis, we are filled with fear and anger, and we hurl those feelings out at God. We may feel that we have been done a grave injustice, that God has made our lives a painful obstacle course and has now sat back to watch us struggle. Others of us may feel uncomfortable getting angry at God, so we turn our anger inward. We blame ourselves. "We are so hopeless and insignificant, we are such spiritual failures that God wouldn't bother with us. Why should God answer *our* prayers in any sort of specific way?"

Both of these very natural attitudes block our prayers for healing and belie a lack of faith in God's goodness and care. If we seek healing without starting from the foundation of faith, we will be frustrated and confused. Faith is not some magical quality that we pump up by the force of our emotions: "I think he can, I think he can, I think he can," like the little engine that could. Faith is a gift from God. God is not interested in our fancy words; God is interested in our honesty. And even if we are having a hard time getting past the ways we feel toward God, simply telling that to God is a faithful prayer and a good place to start. We start where we are.

Trusting God means opening our hearts to God's love and power even when the circumstances of our lives do not seem very fair. Once we are willing to do that—and we must do that again and again—we can begin to participate with Christ in his healing ministry. There is no magic formula to make God's healing "work." There is only One who bids us to come along on the journey.

&

The healing ministry brought John back into the Christian community. Though he was raised in a Christian home, his commitment to God had been minimal. Then, in college, he had a dream that opened up an entirely new spiritual reality for him and transformed his life.

It was a simple dream. John saw himself as he believed God saw him, both as a young man and an old man. He was dressed in a robe of light, able to give and receive God's abundant love. For a while, he walked virtually alone in this new spiritual journey. Though he sought to make real in his life the power and presence of God that was revealed to him in his dream, he did not have the desire to join with the Christian community, nor was he comfortable affirming the basic beliefs of Christianity. He felt an inability to believe in Jesus. But when he saw a healing conference advertised at the local parish church, he decided to attend. It was sponsored by the Order of St. Luke the Physician of America, an ecumenical movement committed to the restoration of the healing ministry among the churches. At the conference he learned of steps he could take to help him to walk in God's healing power.

The first step was the removal of obstacles that were blocking John's receiving God's power, an honest and thorough housecleaning, a willingness to admit and let go of anything that was standing in the way of a deeper communion with God. At the conference they did this by individually writing out those blocks or sins in their own lives, offering them to God by placing them on the altar and being set free of them, knowing the papers would be burned by the minister.

The second step was receiving the power by simply asking for God's healing to come into those places of need. The participants had the opportunity to do this when they were invited to come forward to the altar and receive the laying on of hands and prayers for healing. John went forward for healing prayers and was disappointed when the powerful and persuasive leader of the conference went to pray for people on the other side of the rail while the ordinary and bumbling parish priest came to pray for him. He finally came to realize that God was either in this process or not, and that one final block he needed to remove was the way he expected God to touch him. Could God's power be as present in the ordinary and bumbling as it seemed to be in the dramatic and charismatic?

When his turn came, John asked for the ability to believe in Jesus. There were no bells or heavenly choirs, and John will always remember the peculiar expression on the priest's face when he made his request. Yet within two weeks, John found a growing sense of comfort about Jesus. He was given the gift of being able to believe that Jesus was who he said he was.

The third step taught at the healing conference was releasing the power, walking in the new reality which God's healing power was bringing about. For John, this was not only a matter of discovering that he now believed in Jesus, but also discovering that God's healing power could be in the church. He joined with others who had participated in the healing conference, and together they formed a chapter of the Order of St. Luke. The group studied the healing stories in the Gospels and the Book of Acts and began actively participating in the healing ministry, carrying what they learned to others through prayer. It was through this experience that John came into the Christian community as an adult.

These simple steps—the removal of blocks, the receiving of power, the releasing of power—are one way to enter the healing process. They are not the only way, they are simply a description of a process that many people have found helpful in entering into God's healing presence. The removal of blocks is a spiritual housecleaning that can be done through writing in a journal, through preparation for the sacrament of confession, or through a "fourth step inventory"—the thorough and honest moral inventory suggested in the twelve-step programs of Alcoholics Anonymous and other recovery groups. Wisdom and experience have shown that, although confessing your sins to God in solitude is possible and effective, most of us need the tangible, objective experience of opening our hearts and souls to another human being. Such an experience often brings a release and a self-acceptance that could not have been realized alone.

Receiving the power begins by asking the question, "Where is the healing ministry of God most needed in my own life?" By asking God to come and transform however he chooses, the question enables us to bring our needs to God in the spirit of trust that God can meet us in a loving way. We can only bring our needs to God. It is not our responsibility in the healing process, nor is it helpful, for us to try and dictate to God how our needs should be met. In this step of receiving, it is better to express our needs in the context of the gathered community, so that others may be channels of God's healing touch.

Releasing the power is walking forth in the knowledge that Christ is present and that we can participate with him in this healing work. It is not a frenzied activism based on trying to bring about a certain result by the force of our willful believing, but rather an active and continual resting in the sure knowledge that God is present as healer, and that we may be invited to share in this ministry.

&

One of the stories in the Bible shows us how Jesus became known as healer in a very difficult family setting.

> And when Jesus had crossed again in the boat to the other side, a great crowd gathered about him; and he was beside the sea. Then came one of the rulers of the synagogue, Jairus by name; and seeing him, he fell at his feet, and besought him, saying, "My little daughter is at the point of death. Come and lay your hands on her, so that she may be made well, and live." And he went with him.
>
> [As he travelled to Jairus's house, Jesus was interrupted by a woman seeking healing.]
>
> While he was still speaking, there came from the ruler's house some who said, "Your daughter is dead. Why trouble the Teacher any further?" But ignoring what they said, Jesus said to the ruler of the synagogue, "Do not fear, only believe." And he allowed no one to follow him except Peter and James and John the brother of James. When they came to the house of the ruler of the synagogue, he saw a tumult, and people weeping and wailing loudly. And when he had entered, he said to them, "Why do you make a tumult and weep? The child is not dead but sleeping." And they laughed at him. But he put them all outside, and took the child's father and mother and those who were with him, and went in where the child was. Taking her by the hand he said to her, "Talitha cumi"; which means, "Little girl, I say to you, arise." And immediately the girl got up and walked (she was twelve years of age), and they were immediately overcome with amazement. And he strictly charged them that no one should know this, and told them to give her something to eat.   —Mark 5:21-24, 35-43

Clearly, Jairus had a tender and deep love for his daughter. Her serious illness was the catalyst that brought him to Jesus. We wonder if this synagogue official would have ever seen Jesus face to face had his heart not been broken by the suffering of his child.

Certainly, Jesus was a questionable character. He was much more popular among the uneducated and those on the borderline of society—the tax collectors, prostitutes, lepers. They were the kind of people that did not always support Jairus's synagogue. Indeed, most of the scribes and teachers of the synagogue had grave doubts about the orthodoxy of Jesus' theology.

Most likely, Jairus had been in on some of the discussions. But whatever reservations he may have had, he must have worked through them and let go of them before setting out to find Jesus, for in the gospel story we see a man in the midst of a large crowd unabashedly throwing himself at Jesus' feet and asking for help with the certain faith that Jesus' touch could heal his daughter.

How did he know? What wrestling went on within his heart and within his household as he deliberated over what to do for his ailing child? What kind of stories had he heard about Jesus' power to heal? Was it faith or was it desperation that brought him to his knees? When a father looks into the face of his suffering child and sees his own powerlessness, where does he turn?

Leaving his daughter behind in the care of others, perhaps never to see her alive again, Jairus admitted defeat and set out to find help outside of himself, outside of his familiar, predictable environment. Jairus set out to find Jesus. After making his way through the crowds and spotting Jesus, he simply yet boldly made his request known: "My little daughter is at the point of death. Come and lay your hands on her, so that she may be made well, and live." He did not try to show Jesus his credentials or prove to him why his daughter deserved his special attention. He simply fell at Jesus' feet and asked for help.

And Jesus responded by going home with this man who had sought him out. He stopped what he was doing, changed his plans for the day, and headed off with this desperate father. What a surge of hope this must have brought to Jairus.

But then Jesus stopped to deal with a needy woman who had approached him surreptitiously. The gospel does not say what Jairus was thinking, but it records the disciples' impatience. Certainly precious moments were being lost. And how that father's heart must have sunk when the word came to him, "Your daughter is dead. Why trouble the Teacher any further?" The cold wave of fear, shock, and grief was engulfing him when Jesus cut it short. "Do not fear, only believe."

What a preposterous thing for Jesus to say! Only believe what? That the impossible could be real? That death was not final? Jairus had a choice here—either he could accept the advice of the household messenger and send Jesus away, or he could keep walking with him.

It was at this point that Jesus singled out his three closest disciples to accompany him—Peter, James, and John. Perhaps it was their simple obedience and willingness to follow Jesus, even into a house filled with death, that gave Jairus the courage to continue on with Jesus in the face of the absurdly impossible, to brush past the mourners who were laughing at Jesus, and to bring Jesus and his disciples into his home. Here Jairus was joined by his wife, and together they gazed at the lifeless body of the child they had begotten and raised. And they watched in amazement as Jesus simply and tenderly took the girl by the hand and said, "Talitha cumi."

The actual Aramaic words are preserved in the gospel account, no doubt passed on to the gospel writer by an eyewitness. Those words of Jesus that quickened the lifeless body of their child must have been forever branded in the memories and hearts of that mother and father. The gospel says that they were overcome with amazement, but Jesus, in his simple and down-to-earth way, was concerned that the girl be given something to eat. Life goes on in a home, even when Jesus is in its midst, and a growing girl needs her nourishment.

&

How do we seek healing for our children and for ourselves? How do we turn to Jesus in our powerlessness? How do we seek him out in the crowd and bring him into our home?

If the whole idea of seeking spiritual healing is strange and new to us, it may be helpful to recognize the ways that we are already welcoming Jesus into our home as healer, the ways that the ministry of healing can already be found in our daily activities.

Every time we kiss a hurt finger, give a hug after a hard day, or lay a hand on a burning forehead, we are participating with Christ in his desire to bring healing to our homes. The same Lord who has called our family into being is present with us, nurturing all that is good and whole and life-giving.

There are little ways that we can begin to affirm Jesus as healer in our midst—by laying hands on sick family members and praying for Jesus' healing presence along with our regular regimen of aspirin and trips to the doctor, by asking the community prayer chain to pray for us in times of need, by seeking the sacramental support of our priests or ministers during times of illness. When we know of others who are ill, we can pray for them as a family. Thus our children will see that spiritual healing is an ordinary part of the Christian life. All of these actions will encourage a climate of faith and hopefulness in our home and a willingness to take the next step in the journey of healing.

If your church community does not have healing services or an active healing ministry, you could do some exploring in your area and find a place where Christ's healing ministry is being offered. We drive fifty minutes to share in such a community.

The need of one of our children prodded us to grow deeper in our understanding of the healing ministry. Although we both had participated in healing prayer before, when the needs were great within our own family, we had difficulty sustaining the faith and commitment needed to consistently intercede on behalf of our child. While we theoretically always believed in God's concern for our situation and in God's power to heal, we were hesitant to actively seek healing for our son who was born deaf.

We had read about grieving parents dragging their deaf child from one faith healer to another, never able to love and accept the child as he was. And we did not want to use the hope for healing as a way of denying the severity of Nathan's handicap, nor did we want him to feel that he was somehow unacceptable to us because he could not hear. Yet it may have been that we were afraid of being disappointed, so we did not allow ourselves to articulate to God how much we would like for our son to be able to hear. We prayed for courage, for patience, for wisdom. It was safer that way.

But the gospel stories of Jesus' opening ears and eyes continued to tug at our hearts. When we heard of a dramatic healing in a nearby church community, we began to meet with the priest there and to begin a journey in healing that is still in process. We were struck with the gentle and open spirit among those who were called into this ministry of prayer for healing. And we sensed their firm conviction that Christ was present to heal, and that our task was to participate with him in this ministry. The community did not seek to dictate to God the "the correct way" of healing our son. Nor did they attempt to manipulate us into believing harder or believing a certain way. There was only the willingness to walk along with us as we sought Jesus' healing for our son.

Nathan has been receiving "soaking prayer" from various members of this prayer team for over six months now. It consists of the laying-on-of-hands for extended periods several times a week and quiet prayer to join in Jesus' healing work. The results have been remarkable.

We cannot separate between the healing that is a result of the prayers and the healing that is the result of simple growth or the good work of teachers and counselors at his school. Jesus uses all these means in his work of healing. Nathan still cannot hear, but he is much calmer and more communicative. He is making friends and is learning to read. Six months ago his school did not want to continue working with him because he was unteachable, now they are marvelling at his eagerness to learn.

We are grateful for the chance to walk with others in this healing journey, to learn more and more each day how to let Jesus as healer into our home. There have been so many unexpected healings brought to our entire family as the result of actively seeking the healing presence of Christ.

We no longer see Nathan and his needs as the focus of our family; we see Christ as the center. We pray more often for both of our children now, as they sleep, as they go off to school. Betsy has known a deep healing in the way she recalls Nathan's difficult birth experience. She has been able to invite Christ into those memories, and she has known a real release from guilt and anxiety.

We have both felt more freedom and boldness to pray for others who might come to us. Because we have been challenged to see Christ's wholeness for our family, we are able to challenge others to do the same.

The journey is not over, nor has it been without its pitfalls. There have been times of disappointment and discouragement, times of difficulty in scheduling and making connections, times of hearing conflicting messages as each of us seeks to discern the voice of the Lord. But throughout the questioning that arises, a quiet confidence has grown within us that Christ will continue to bring healing and wholeness for the entire family through the loving prayer of the community gathered in his name.

&

Jesus had a wonderful way of physically reaching out to those who came to him in need—laying his hands on twisted bodies, touching the untouchable, taking a child by the hand, making mud from spit and dirt to put on the eyes of a blind man. He was not afraid of the dirt and smell and closeness of this earth.

Perhaps Jesus learned about intimacy and wholeness from those closest to him. When he fell down and skinned his knees in the streets of Nazareth, his mother's hands washed away the dirt and dried the tears. When the saw slipped as he learned carpentry alongside his father, Joseph's strong hands stopped the bleeding, bound up the wound, and encouraged him to keep trying.

But as a grown man, when Jesus hung bleeding on the cross, no one was there to bind his wounds or comfort him. Yet from that place of total vulnerability and powerlessness, he reached out to comfort the one who had borne him. When he saw his mother at the foot of the cross, he entrusted her to the care of the beloved disciple. The healing that he brought for her, and for every one of us, at the cross could not be administered directly. It was through the tender care of the community that Mary's broken heart was healed. By God's grace, in this moment of extreme difficulty for Mary and John, they were able to actively reach out and receive that healing.

May we likewise find a place in Christ's community where we can come to receive the healing touch of the resurrected Lord.

Seven

Open Hands

VERY EARLY IN OUR JOURNEY AS PARENTS, even while our first child was still in the womb, we learned what it means to trust and to offer our child to God.

Halfway through that first pregnancy, premature labor began, and Betsy was rushed to the hospital. She called John, who was at his first day of clinical chaplaincy training at another hospital, and he met Betsy in her room. We talked and prayed together as we awaited the surgery, in which the doctors would attempt to keep the baby from being born so early. The chances of survival for such a premature infant would be very slim.

John had written a song earlier that year, before we had conceived this child, about how each painful experience is an opportunity to learn new steps in the dance of life with God. One of the verses was about a couple who had lost a child and had grown angry and bitter. The child was dancing joyfully with God, but the parents had refused to keep dancing through the pain. We felt that the song was happening to us. We knew that this child was a precious gift. With anguish we let go together, knowing that God's ways are not our ways.

In surgery, the doctors tipped Betsy nearly upside-down to relieve the pressure on her cervix, which had begun dilating three and a half months before the due date. She asked for only local anesthesia so that she could be aware of what was happening with the baby. As she was taking deep breaths and praying the name of Jesus, John was in another room calling friends in the Christian community to enlist their prayer support. As John hung up the phone and joined in prayer, he sensed God saying, "What do you want?" And he knew that because this was God speaking, he could say what he wanted with complete trust and confidence. "I want the child to live," was his reply, and he immediately sensed that God was saying, "The child will live." His grateful response was to offer the child back again to God: "His (or her) name is yours." And as John spoke these words, he knew that this must be the child's name.

When John met Betsy in the recovery room, his first words were, "How do you say 'His name is yours' in Hebrew?" She thought he had gone crazy, until she heard his story. We let go of our ideas of an Anna, Rachel, or Abraham and spent the rest of the pregnancy experimenting with the possible combinations in Hebrew. Several months later when our little one came out full-term and healthy, we embraced Shemaleiah, which means "Her name belongs to the Lord." Her name is a constant reminder that she is a gift we hold with open hands as we entrust her to God's care.

&

Another parent in a much different time and culture learned a similar lesson in a more dramatic situation. After a long and tense time, Abraham finally saw God's promise fulfilled. He had a son by his own wife, Sarah. Then, in one of the most powerful and poignant narratives in the Hebrew scriptures, we read of Abraham's "testing." "Take your son, your only son Isaac, whom you love, and go to the land of Moriah, and offer him there as a burnt offering upon one of the mountains of which I shall tell you" (Genesis 22:2).

We all recall the happy ending to the story, that the angel of the Lord stayed Abraham's hand and provided a ram for the sacrifice, and we may have learned that this story was important to the Hebrews because it established the fact that God did not desire child sacrifice as did the surrounding pagan gods. Still, most parents are horrified when they read this story because we intuitively sense the same harsh demands upon us. We too are called to let go of our children, entrusting them into God's care.

Abraham did not choose to trust God with the fate of his son in one dramatic moment of faithfulness. His life had been filled with smaller steps of trusting obedience, along with a fair share of doubts and struggles. When he was an old man, well-established in his community, he was willing to launch into the unknown in response to God's call: "Go from your country and your kindred and your father's house to the land that I will show you" (Genesis 12:1). Later, when Abraham's flocks and those of his nephew Lot became too numerous, Abraham trusted God's provision enough to offer his nephew the pick of the land and for himself to settle elsewhere. When he and Sarah heard the preposterous and laughable message of the angelic visitors, that they, long past the years of child-bearing, would conceive a son, they trusted enough to at least give it a try, and again they found that God was, indeed, the kind of God they could rely on.

All these experiences of God's provision and mercy enabled Abraham to make that most difficult and faithful decision on Mt. Moriah. Even when everything told him that to kill Isaac was absurd—this was the very child who was to carry on the covenant promise of descendents as numerous as the stars—he was willing to let go of his perceptions of how God should fulfill the promises in order to embrace God. Nothing was more important to Abraham than God.

And we modern parents are challenged to meet God with that same radical trust. We must not let our perceptions of God's blessing, God's covenant, or God's promise stand in the way of our single-minded devotion to God himself. It is a form of idolatry to cherish those good gifts that God gives more than cherishing God. And this subtle idolatry is so often nurtured in our homes. Not only do we play god when we try to over-control the lives of our children, but we also make our children into little gods. We worship them by devoting all our attention and energy to them and make their success the barometer of our happiness and self worth.

&

We are challenged to trust God and to let go of our children each time we allow our children to break away from us and take those needed steps of growth—getting on the bus for kindergarden, staying overnight at a friend's, driving the car, going away to college. Sometimes the letting go is easy.

At other times, it is extremely difficult. But the conscious choice to invite God into the process will certainly bring perspective to the entire family.

We recently talked to a man whose oldest child was about to leave for college. With tears in his eyes, the father told us that the entire family had totally avoided the subject of the impending departure until about one week before. Suddenly, in the middle of the meal, the father stopped everyone and said that he wanted to say grace. He thanked God for the food, for his family, and especially for his son who was soon to go out and make his way in the world. A somberness settled on the family for the rest of the meal as they finally admitted the intensity of feelings they shared about the upcoming departure. The father had sensed that they all needed God's help in letting go. They were not a family that prayed together regularly, but on the rare occasions that they did, it was around the table for grace at special meals. Never mind that this was an ordinary weekday meal and that it was already half over, they managed to seize the opportunity, and because of it they were all able to trust God a little more and to reach out to one another a little better.

Sometimes letting go is traumatic and heart-wrenching—when a child must be sent away to a special school because his or her needs cannot be met locally, when a teen-ager is sent to a rehabilitation center to deal with alcohol or substance abuse, when accident or illness seriously impairs the potential and capability of a child. We have friends, faithful, committed, and loving people, who had to make the very difficult decision to turn their son out of their home until he could show them that he had made significant lifestyle changes. They continue to love and keep in contact with their son as he goes in and out of jail, standing ready to support any steps of growth he may choose to take, but they have ceased to be manipulated and held emotional hostage by his erratic behavior. This letting go was a process of deep grief, especially for the mother. She went through all the old baby pictures, all the childhood memories, as she released this troubled young man, entrusting him to God's mercy, knowing that she may never see him alive again. And out of the suffering has come a new freedom for the rest of the family, a refocusing on God and a renewed sense of the importance of placing God at the center of their family rather than the needs of one child.

Whether the process of letting go is long or short, smooth or rocky, there often comes with it a sense of relief and freedom. Finally, one has to let go of the impossible task of making the members of one's family perfect or of feeling responsible for every individual's happiness. What a relief it is to realize that we are not God!

&

Learning to trust requires that we identify and overcome the fears that are blocking our growth. Look at the story of one who overcame his fears and learned to trust Jesus more fully.

> Then he [Jesus] made the disciples get into the boat and go before him to the other side, while he dismissed the crowds. And after he had dismissed the crowds, he went up on the mountain by himself to pray. When evening came, he was there alone, but the boat by this time was many furlongs distant from the land, beaten by the waves; for the wind was against them. And in the fourth watch of the night he came to them, walking on the sea. But when the disciples saw him walking on the sea, they were terrified, saying, "It is a ghost!" And they cried out for fear. But immediately he spoke to them, saying, "Take heart, it is I; have no fear."

And Peter answered him, "Lord, if it is you, bid me come to you on the water." He said, "Come." So Peter got out of the boat and walked on the water and came to Jesus; but when he saw the wind, he was afraid, and beginning to sink he cried out, "Lord, save me." Jesus immediately reached out his hand and caught him, saying to him, "O man of little faith, why did you doubt?" And when they got into the boat, the wind ceased. And those in the boat worshiped him, saying, "Truly you are the Son of God." —Matthew 14:22-33

It had been a long and wearying stretch of days for Jesus and his disciples. They had heard the discouraging news about the beheading of John the Baptist, and when they tried to get away for a time, the crowds had followed after their boat on the shore, greeting them with their clamoring needs when they set foot on land. Jesus, having just miraculously fed this throng of over five thousand, must have sensed the disciples' need for a time apart, a time of rest. So he sent them across the lake in the privacy of their boat, while he himself stayed and dismissed the crowd. When the last of his followers had been sent on their way, Jesus took some precious moments alone to go up the mountain to pray. In the darkness, a sudden storm arose on the sea below him. The disciples were in the midst of it with still several hours to go before dawn. A time of rest had begun to turn into a nightmare. And Jesus came to them in their need, very simply and directly, walking on the water.

Now these friends of Jesus had become accustomed to extraordinary events—they had witnessed marvelous healings, they had seen him feed the multitude with only five loaves and two fish, and they had even seen Jesus calm a storm such as this one once before. But this appearance went beyond those earlier events. Certainly those other events showed that Jesus was an extraordinary person, but this business of walking on the waves of a storm showed Jesus to be totally outside of their human realm of experience. The disciples were terrified. They thought they were being approached by an unpredictable creature from another world: "It is a ghost!" they cried out in fear. A sudden storm on the sea at night is scary enough, but an unnatural apparition from nowhere is even more terrifying.

Yet the words of Jesus ring out through the dark and confusion, "Take heart, it is I; have no fear." And those words touch a place of recognition, of comfort, deep within them. Is this the same voice of the one who tells them parables as they sit around their evening fire? Is this the same voice of the one who rebukes demons and speaks gently to little children? Is this Jesus' voice coming to them in the darkness of the storm?

Sometimes our perceptions of God and how God communicates with us are shaken by the real life storms in which we find ourselves. This doesn't seem to be the kind of life we bargained for when we started following God's way. And the phantoms in the darkness befuddle us. How can we trust someone who seems to be a ghost? What is faith and what is foolishness?

Peter must have struggled with these questions, but there was something familiar about that voice. Peter is the first to act. "Lord, if it is you, bid me come to you on the water." When the word returns to him, "Come," he must have felt certain that this is the voice of Jesus calling to him. He can trust that voice as he has grown to respect and love the man who called him to leave his fishing nets and follow. Peter steps out of the boat and starts walking to Jesus on the water. Then a gust of wind reminds him of his whereabouts, and he loses his footing and begins sinking into the water. As he cries out to Jesus for help, Jesus reaches down to him and soon they are safely in the boat again. And all the disciples are gripped with a profoundly new perception of who this Jesus is they have come to know.

The comfort of recognizing Jesus' voice gave Peter the courage to step out onto the water. But he was overcome with fear again when he saw the wind. He was overwhelmed by the circumstances of his situation and his trust turned to panic as he began to sink. His reaction was totally understandable. Who would not panic upon the realization that they are standing outside of the boat in the middle of a dark, windy storm? What modern-day parents do not panic as they stand in the midst of the storms of drug abuse, AIDS, teen pregnancies, and child abuse? Yet Jesus' gentle rebuke to Peter, "O man of little faith, why do you doubt?" also chides us as he draws us out of our panic and into the safety of his presence.

How is it that we grow more trusting of God in the midst of the storms of family life? How can we trust someone who seems as if he might be a ghost? Just as Peter discerned the true identity of the ghostly figure by recognizing Jesus' familiar voice, so we each have the opportunity of getting to know Jesus' voice through the words of the Gospels and through the worship and fellowship of the Christian community. By getting to know Jesus' voice in these settings, we will be able to recognize him when he calls to us in unfamiliar ways. What might begin with a shadowy image will become clearer and clearer as his living word speaks to us.

&

John had such an experience when he was preparing for his ordination to the diaconate and looking for his first job in ministry. The direction he was to take would deeply affect the entire family. He kept sensing from God that he was to find a position where he would be in charge of a congregation. The message sounded like nonsense to him. A newly ordained deacon does not often start out with a church of his own. Was this word a ghostly apparition sprung from his own anxieties and desires?

He continued to pray and to sense the same message. He shared it with his closest friend from seminary who encouraged him to trust the voice he was hearing and to wait expectantly. Soon after, further confirmation came through his diocesan bishop. This man, a man not wont to mystical revelations, called John and said he had a dream that John should be at St. Luke's. St. Luke's did consider John and indeed called him to be their rector even before he had been ordained deacon. Days later, as John was walking in the procession into the cathedral for his ordination, one of the wardens of St. Luke's met him with the thumbs up sign, assuring him that he was called to minister in St. Luke's. What started out as a vague, uncertain perception in prayer had indeed turned out to be God's call.

At important junctures—a move, a career change, the commitment to a relationship—we often are consciously listening for the voice of God. But it is in the less than momentous events of family life that we can cultivate an openness to God. In stormy battles of wills—over chores, homework, bedtimes—perhaps Jesus is walking by, calling to us, asking us to step out and trust that he can transform the battleground. It may seem as crazy as stepping out of a boat in a storm to tell a joke in the middle of a heated argument, or to call "time out" for a walk in the woods, but sometimes the promptings to do such things are the voice of God. And sometimes they are just what is needed to bring relief and healing to frustrating circumstances.

&

How do we remove the barriers that keep us from trusting God? Before we can overcome obstacles, we need to identify them. We need the honesty, humility, and willingness to honestly answer the question, "What has really become the center of our family?"

Families often tend to focus on one member with a particular need. If a child has a behavior or learning problem at school, all the emotional energy of the family is often poured into that issue. When a parent is unemployed or depressed, the rest of the family often focuses on the malaise of that parent, trying doubly hard not to upset or offend, trying to cushion him or her from the pain that may be the needed impetus to keep growing. When one member has an alcohol problem, the others often cover for him or her, only supporting the denial that is part of the disease. It is a natural reaction for a family to focus inward, to be constellated around the greatest perceived need. But such self-absorption is deadly to the spirit.

Once we can identify and name that which has become the center of our family life, that which has pushed God out, we can begin to let go and to welcome God back to the center of our family. There is a joyous relief at giving up the game of playing God, of trying to fix everyone. There is a freedom in throwing open the door to any possibility, trusting that Jesus' familiar voice will lead us in the right direction.

We foster trust by trusting and by sharing that confidence with our children. Betsy will always remember her mother's strong faith that God would provide for their large family. Even when the end of the month came and they were eating lots of beans and potatoes, they never doubted that they would be fed and cared for. Sweets were a very rare treat for their household, and during one of those lean times, Betsy remembers her mother discovering a whole bag of candy under the sink. Her mother insisted that she had not put it there, but that God must have wanted to surprise them with a little treat! Her faith and trust in God's provision and her good humor were effectively communicated. Because of this strong example, to this day Betsy finds it a very easy and natural thing to trust God's provision in financial matters. When we keep an open heart in our relationship with God, always asking him to show us places where we have not put him in the center, then we are more apt to pass on to our children an attitude of trust rather than fear.

&

Mary and Joseph certainly had much that they could have been fearful about in their early family life.

The circumstances of the pregnancy must have seemed a bit questionable to many. Then there was the long trip to Bethlehem during those last wearying days of waiting and the birth of their child in a stable, with no relatives or friends to throw a baby shower or offer support and congratulations.

But rather than turning inward and growing fearful, Mary and Joseph opened their hearts to the unfamiliar guests who sought out their child—the local shepherds, the Magi from distant lands, the elderly prophetess Anna, the faithful Simeon.

And then came the strange angelic warning in a dream, that they must flee the country immediately to avoid the slaughter by Herod's troops. Did they have time to test that voice, to talk about it, to pray together? Or did they take off that very night? Joseph was acquainted with God's word coming through a dream, that is how his inner turmoil about Mary's pregnancy had been resolved. I wonder if Mary had the dream as well, or chose to trust her husband's direction.

A woman longs for her mother at the time she first gives birth. For Mary to wrap up her newborn and take off into the night in the opposite direction from all that was safe and familiar must have been very difficult.

A man longs to provide security and comfort for his growing family. For Joseph to lead them off into the wilderness toward a strange country with no guarantee of welcome or livelihood must have been very unsettling.

Yet ancient Egypt had often been a place of refuge for the chosen people. Ancient legends about the flight into Egypt tell of how the holy family was protected from dragons, revered by lions and leopards, hidden from Herod's pursuing troops by spiders spinning their webs over the mouth of their cave, and fed by palm trees that bent before them to share their fruit.

Sometimes God's call cuts across all that is natural to us—a mother's and father's instincts, a child's needs—yet the amazing provision in the wilderness reminds us that the word of God that calls us to step out into the unfamiliar is a word that we can trust.

May we have the willingness to trust God's word, however it comes, and the faithfulness to obey. And may we as parents, as we journey in faith with our families, come to more fully entrust and offer our children back to God.

Eight

The Wings of Prayer

WHEN A MAN AND A WOMAN FALL IN LOVE, their affection for one another may be a sudden passionate revelation or a gradual awareness that creeps up and takes them by surprise.

But whatever the pace and style of the courtship, lovers take great delight in spending time together. Whether the setting is a fancy dinner dance or a spontaneous walk around the neighborhood, a trip to the laundromat or a late-night phone conversation, the wonder of sharing deeply and honestly with another person brings energy, joy, and purpose.

We pray in response to the pursuit of our divine lover. Our longing for God and a relationship with God through prayer may seem to appear suddenly at a dramatic turning in our lives. Then again, it may be the result of a gradual awareness of our own inner restlessness and the abundance of God's good gifts to us. Some of us may not yet have begun this journey.

Prayer is first and foremost an opportunity to be honest with the One who knows us better than we know ourselves and loves us fully and perfectly. It has been called "a holy wasting of time," and its purpose is no more lofty and grand than simply wanting to spend time with the one we love. We do ourselves a grave disservice when we think of prayer as something totally foreign to our everyday existence, something that must be done in a holy place with special words and religious feelings accompanying it. To the believer, prayer can be as natural and as normal as breathing.

There is a line in one of John's songs, "I believe in Jesus like a bird believes in wings." So also with prayer. Just as a bird soars through the skies without much thought for how or why its wings are functioning, so the believer can discover prayer lifting and energizing all of life, a natural and integral part of every day.

But for many of us, our images and ideals of what we think prayer should be, and what we think family prayer should be, keep us stuck on the ground, afraid to take off in this spiritual adventure of communicating with God through prayer. Perhaps we have had a wise old patriarch or matriarch who prayed eloquent prayers at family gatherings. Our own stumbling attempts pale in comparison, so we don't even try. Or perhaps we have been turned off by a piety that seems artificial or unreal, by being forced to go to confession or to memorize long and tedious Bible passages that we had to recite at family prayer times. It may well be that, in reaction, we come to find ourselves steering clear of any formal praying in the home.

If we are to grow spiritually, it is important that we be willing to identify and let go of the perceptions of what we think family prayer should or might be, and together with God forge a realistic relationship that is natural and real. However a family's prayer life develops, we may find that the first attempts are difficult and uncomfortable. Something new often takes extra patience and courage.

&

The best place to start in this adventure is right where we are. The scriptures make it abundantly clear that God values an honest and open heart more than the fanciest of formal prayers. Jesus launched his severest criticism against those who hid behind a cloak of religiosity, those who used the formalities of prayer and ritual to close out God's living and active Spirit. The kind of honest prayer to which God responds starts right where we are—with our faith or lack of it, our hesitations, our longings, and our willingness to bring all of these things into our conversation.

The Hebrew scriptures are filled with examples of individuals who spoke to God honestly with all the particular emotions they were feeling. Abraham bargained for the cities of Sodom and Gomorrah, chiding God to be more merciful. Moses complained about the thankless and impossible job he had been given to lead the chosen people. David danced before the Lord in delight as the Ark of the Covenant was brought into Jerusalem. Job shook his fist at heaven for the unfair afflictions he endured.

And the Gospels are filled with examples of Jesus responding patiently to those who came to him with genuine openness. The father who brought his son to be healed was not turned away just because his faith was wavering. "I believe; help my unbelief" was the best prayer he could muster, but Jesus accepted it and him, and offered healing to his son. When Mary and Martha's brother died and Martha met Jesus with recriminations—"Lord, if you had been here my brother would not have died"—Jesus neither turned away from their anger nor attempted to defend himself. Rather, he entered into their grief and took them beyond the hopelessness of their present situation.

There was seemingly no emotion or situation that was inappropriate to bring to Jesus. Jesus valued the opportunity to meet and touch people exactly as they were, where they were. It was those who were out to prove their point and trip him up with clever questions that he turned away or refused to answer. The starting place for all prayer is an honest and straightforward expression of who we are and what we are experiencing.

Besides meeting people with specific needs, Jesus spent extensive time with a small group of followers. There must have been numerous conversations with him that went unrecorded. Several that are recorded hint at the gentle unfolding that must have been going on all around him.

When Jesus' disciples were perplexed about a story or teaching they had heard, they would often ask for an explanation, and he would clarify the meaning or implications of his teaching. Even when Jesus' disciples were filled with competitive and self-aggrandizing thoughts, ones they shared with Jesus—"Grant us to sit, one at your right hand and one at your left, in your glory"—he was not shocked and critical, but rather he gently redirected their focus. These holy conversations, when people came to Jesus with intense, diverse feelings and thoughts and found themselves accepted, challenged, and redirected, must have been special times. Yet they took place in such ordinary fashion. Everyday issues were transformed as the conversation drew each member beyond his limited understanding.

Such prayerful conversations can happen in our homes and families today. It may be something as simple as a discussion of the needs in the neighborhood or a lighthearted conversation about what we would do if Jesus suddenly walked through the front door. It may be as intense as discussing what our funeral plans are or what we most value and cherish about each other. These are not times for one member to dominate the conversation or for another to get on a soapbox about a favorite issue, but rather a chance for all to respond together to how God may be making himself known. God is to be found in these holy conversations, and a conscious awareness of God's presence can enrich the life of every family member.

&

There are, of course, the examples of Jesus' own prayer from scripture. Luke 4:16 tells us that Jesus "went to the synagogue, as his custom was, on the Sabbath day." Jesus' personal prayer was rooted in the liturgical prayer of his people. Even when he received a cool response from the religious leaders, there is good evidence to suggest that he continued to attend synagogue regularly, to join his prayers with those of the community, and to teach as the opportunity arose.

Jesus also frequently found time to go off by himself for special periods of prayer. Before launching on his preaching tour "in the morning, a great while before day, he rose and went out to a lonely place, and there he prayed" (Mark 1:35). He also drew apart for special prayer times before choosing the twelve disciples, before his transfiguration, after feeding the multitudes, and, most significantly, in the Garden of Gethsemane the night before his death. Jesus knew that God had a direction and purpose for his life, and at times of decision or crisis he withdrew to affirm that identity and direction. When all those around him were questioning who he was and placing their own demands and expectations upon him, he needed time apart in a quiet space to peacefully accept and acknowledge his true identity in God.

In fact it may well have been this regular practice of prayer that prompted his disciples to ask for direction in their own praying.

> He was praying in a certain place, and when he ceased, one of his disciples said to him, "Lord, teach us to pray, as John taught his disciples."   —Luke 11:1-2

Jesus responded to this request by teaching his disciples a prayer which has come to be called the "Lord's Prayer." Books and treatises, sermons and songs have been written about the Lord's Prayer. Certainly its beauty and wisdom are expansive. But what can it teach us about prayer in a contemporary family?

The Lord's Prayer teaches us with bold directness to address our God as father. An intimacy and reciprocity is assumed; the one whom we address in prayer yearns to be in a relationship with us and with our families. It teaches us simplicity. In a few precise words, God's sovereignty is affirmed and our physical, spiritual, and social needs are brought before God. It shows us what Jesus thought our priorities should be. Our first concerns must be God's concerns—to hallow God's name, to see God's kingdom come by doing his will here on earth—and then our needs for sustenance, harmonious relationships, and deliverance in times of trial fall into place. The order of the petitions in this prayer is a good example of Jesus' teaching to "seek first his kingdom and his righteousness, and all these things shall be yours as well" (Matthew 6:33).

Finally, the Lord's Prayer teaches us that in the simple ordinary working out of our lives together before God, we are bringing the kingdom into the present. As we invite the intimate presence of our father God into our daily family life, we will see his Spirit powerfully transforming this earthly existence. As we eat our bread thankfully, acknowledging the creator's hand, we will be tasting the messianic banquet. As we forgive our spouse or children for a foolish word or a thoughtless action, we are allowing God's forgiveness to cleanse and prepare us for that final reckoning that will be made at the end of time.

In this short prayer, Jesus shows us the simplicity, directness, and priorities that can help shape our family prayers.

&

But how do we begin? How do we pray in the midst of our own doubts and uncertainties? And how do we take the giant leap from praying on our own to beginning to pray as a family?

First, we need to realize that prayer is one of the most foolish, yet valuable things we can do. "Foolish" because it is a "holy wasting of time." In a pragmatic world where seeing is believing and God's presence and reality are unprovable, taking precious time out of our lives to pray may seem naive. There is a bit of the skeptical pragmatist in each of us.

When we were in a rocky portion of our engagement and were spending much time in prayer, both together and apart, seeking God's guidance and reconciliation, John was feeling a particular despair one day. The day's headlines shouted out "China Invades Vietnam," and he thought, The world is falling apart, and I'm wasting all my time praying about this relationship I'm struggling with. The response John felt from God was that just as we were faithful in letting God bring reconciliation between two people, so also would God use that faithfulness for the peace of the rest of the world.

Now that does not mean that when we pray we close our eyes to the needs of the world. It simply means that we must start right where we are in letting God's healing and reconciliation in. Our wasting time with God will transform not only our own lives, but also our world.

We start to pray by setting some time apart, starting perhaps with only five minutes, and by being as honest with God as we can, one day at a time. As we draw near to God, we will find that our desire for prayer will grow, that we will have more of a sense of who we are, and that the fruits of the spirit—love, joy, peace, patience, gentleness, goodness, self-control, faith—will begin to take root in our lives.

These things will not happen without struggle and setbacks. To pray is the work of a lifetime for a Christian.

We can always grow, but holding onto a continual sense of failure is not helpful. For years we have thought that if only we were a bit more organized, disciplined, and spiritually centered, we would be able to pray more consistently and faithfully. What a relief it has been to let go of our perfectionism and just be as honest and faithful as we can one day at a time.

&

When a family begins to pray, it is often easiest to start with the natural rhythms of family life. Many have found bedtime, mealtime, or the time before the family leaves for work and school to be appropriate prayer times. Prayer times should be short, simple, inclusive of all family members, and specifically related to the real world of family life.

Times of family prayer can also arise naturally, spontaneously. When news of a family member's illness or problem arrives in a letter or a phone call, why can we not stop and simply and directly offer that situation up to God? When going on a family trip, we can easily start off the journey with a prayer for safety and for God's blessing. When one family member has a special event—a job interview, a test, or an important meeting—the rest of the family could choose to pray specifically for that situation at the time it is going on. When good news, unexpected gifts, or occasions to celebrate occur, a simple prayer of thanksgiving can be appropriate.

It is often these spontaneous expressions of need or thanks that can pave the way for a more regular and organized prayer time. Rather than feeling guilty about all the ways we are *not* praying, we need to reflect on the ways that we already *are* praying, and open ourselves to take the next steps of growth.

Once the children catch the idea, they often will be teaching us. One day we heard a very upsetting radio news report about children with AIDS in a city near us. The hopelessness of the situation brought tears to our eyes. Our young daughter was also listening and began asking questions.

When the news segment was finished, we turned the radio off and did the best that we could to explain to her the plight of these suffering children. When we finished, she said, "Let's pray for those children who have AIDS." So we took hands and cried and prayed together. Without her suggestion we would have been left in despair. Her directness and simplicity reminded us that there is no darkness or suffering that God cannot penetrate.

As we begin to pray together in our families, the differences in our spiritual personalities soon become obvious. Each parent carries into the marriage various patterns, memories, and expectations that influence his or her understanding of what constitutes a meaningful spirituality. These feelings are often deep and unexamined. It is easy to become judgmental with one another. One partner likes to use formal, structured prayers. The other wants only conversational prayer, and reading prayers from a book feels wrong. One partner wants to say grace at all meals, and the other thinks it is only important at Sunday dinner. It is good to identify the differences and to respect them. Making compromises when needed and giving each other the space to be different are also important.

Exposing the children to a variety of modes of prayer is certainly healthy. We have often described our marriage as being like a rock and a helium balloon tied together. Betsy is the steady, plodding rock that needs to be lightened up by the freedom and spontaneity of the balloon. John could easily fly off into space if not held in place by the steadiness of the rock. Needless to say, Betsy is the more formal and ritualistic of the pair.

It has not always been easy sorting out these differences. When we can let go of the "my way is *really* right and I wish you'd hurry up and realize that" attitude, and accept that God brought us together to learn with and from each other, then we can get on with our spiritual journey together. It also helps us to do a better job of accepting the unique spiritual personalities of each of our children.

Few things are as personal and binding as praying together. What an opportunity we have within our homes to open ourselves to God and to one another in this way!

&

How did Mary and Joseph's unique spiritual personalities help Jesus to unlock his own way of praying and relating to his heavenly father?

Mary was one who reflected on her experiences, pondering over them quietly in her heart. She was open and receptive to God, yet she needed time and space to clarify in her mind what she felt in her heart. Very soon after she received the startling word from Gabriel that she would bear a child, she left her familiar surroundings to go spend time reflecting upon this event with her kinswoman, Elizabeth. She seemed to have had a deep sense of connectedness to history. Her song of praise upon greeting Elizabeth was filled with images of God's goodness and provision throughout the history of her people (Luke 1:46-55). And tradition tells us that it was Mary who recounted to the apostolic writers the stories of Jesus' conception and birth.

Perhaps Jesus learned from his mother about the need for quietness and solitude to clarify and focus a confused or troubled heart. Perhaps she recounted to him the special stories of those strange visitors at his birth, of the meaning of his name, of the puzzling blessing that the aged Simeon gave to him when he was presented in the Temple as a baby. These conversations must have strengthened Jesus' sense of his own identity. Perhaps they also helped open his heart to ponder the mysteries of God's ways.

Joseph was a straightforward and honorable man. He was of the house of David and faithful in keeping God's laws. His faithfulness was expressed in simple obedience. He was a man of action, quick to respond to God's direction. When he found that his betrothed was pregnant, he did what was required by law. He refused to go through with the marriage, but he chose the most merciful and compassionate alternative, to break off the relationship quietly rather than exposing Mary to a public trial that could possibly end in a death penalty. Yet when the angel of the Lord appeared in his dream, and told him of the divine origins of Mary's child, and called him to the task of protecting and caring for the child as his own, he responded by taking Mary home to be his wife and assuming legal responsibility for the child.

A man with less self-confidence and humility could have dismissed such a dream as mere fantasy and walked away from this strange and perplexing family situation. But Joseph's straightforward and faithful relationship to God prepared him to receive God's extraordinary message and to act upon it without delay.

Another angelic messenger in a dream sent Joseph and his new family fleeing to Egypt to escape Herod's sword. His obedience was so clear and decisive that he got up that very night and began the journey. And several years later it was a dream that prompted Joseph to bring his family home to Israel. Joseph was a simple laborer, who fashioned from wood the essentials for this earthly life—a table, a cabinet, a yoke for oxen. Yet his heart was open to dreams, and once he knew God's call he set out to obey.

The scriptures give the impression that Joseph was a man of few words. Yet it seems certain that he conveyed to young Jesus his single-hearted devotion to obeying God's call. Perhaps as they studied the Torah together and read of the fathers of Israel having dreams, Joseph told his son about the angelic messengers who spoke to him.

Certainly, Jesus had the opportunity to make decisive choices to obey God's direction. When he "set his face for Jerusalem," fully aware of the fate that awaited him there, he proceeded faithfully and obediently. And though he wrestled through the night in the Garden of Gethsemane, once he heard God's call reaffirmed, he walked humbly and obediently to the cross on the following morning. His mother and father had received and responded to God's call in very different ways. Their lives of prayer must have touched Jesus very deeply, enabling him to be fully and freely himself as he found his own way of relating and responding to his heavenly father.

As we hold our children on our laps, sit with them around the kitchen table, or write them letters when they are grown and far from home, we can remind them of the stories in their lives that made an impact on who they are, and we can share with them our struggles and joys in this journey of faith.

May we draw them into a life of prayer by taking seriously their dreams and their ponderings and by encouraging them to respond to the Spirit who leads them into a relationship with God.

Nine

Celebrating God's Abundance

WHEN A FAMILY LIVES WITH CHRIST in its midst, there is always reason to celebrate. Jesus came to bring abundant life—"good measure, pressed down, shaken together, running over" (Luke 6:38). Our celebrations are expressions of the joy that this abundant life with God brings, a joy that goes deeper than surface happiness or contentment with the circumstances of one's life. This joy springs from a profound appreciation of life itself, from an acknowledgment of the awesome gift of life, and from the gift of being able to share that life with one another. Finding a rhythm of family prayer that seems to fit your family's needs and personality can take struggle, compromise, and patience. Discovering and creating your own style of celebrating is not always easy either. Ritual and tradition shape us and influence us more deeply than we could ever imagine.

That is why changing the liturgy or style of worship is such a traumatic issue in many churches. The images and pictures that draw us to God and to one another, or have done so in the past, touch deep, often unconscious nerve centers of who we are.

Many a new marriage has barely survived the crises of deciding what kind of Christmas tree to get, whether to open presents on Christmas Eve or Christmas morning, and whose house to go to for Christmas dinner. In establishing our own family practices, it is important to articulate some of our own underlying feelings associated with various customs, to respect the depth of emotion attached to seemingly insignificant actions, and to be flexible enough to let go and to launch out into something new.

The fact that a bit of tinsel, an angel, a star, a certain food on a certain day should move us so deeply is merely testimony that we are rooted in this earth, and that the good gifts of our Creator have a great capacity to delight us. God created us as flesh-and-blood creatures, and we should not despise our connectedness to the things of this earth. True worship and celebration should engage and exhilarate all of our senses, drawing us fully into God's presence. Yet the subtle call of idolatry is very tempting, to worship that which is created, instead of worshiping the Creator. When we focus our attention on the created objects that are the vehicles of delight rather than on the giver of that delight, we cut ourselves off from the living Spirit that undergirds all celebration and that opens our hearts to one another.

We have probably all experienced family celebrations where all the details of the occasion have been attended to, but where there has not been an open-hearted welcoming of God's loving Spirit. As the writer of Proverbs put it, "Better is a dinner of herbs where love is than a fatted ox and hatred with it" (Proverbs 15:17). The most precious parts of any celebration are not the finely polished silver and the heirloom tablecloth, but the unique people sharing that moment with us and the Creator who brought each one into our lives. The objects that have become a part of our celebrations are valuable only insofar as they add to our delight or evoke a story which is part of our shared history—candlesticks given as a wedding present by a grandparent, a Christmas ornament made by little hands years ago, a christening gown worn by generations of ancestors.

As parents, we are responsible for telling those stories that make the objects precious. Just as the people of Israel repeatedly drew hope, joy, and encouragement from recounting the story of God's presence in their midst, and cherished the holy objects they had preserved in the ark of the covenant—the tablets of the law, a bit of manna, Aaron's rod—so it is important for our families to have a sense of our own "salvation history," our own sacred objects and stories that bring tears and laughter and the assurance that God has been working in our midst for a long, long time.

When we can link our own private family stories with the stories of God's salvation in all times and places, then the delight and joy in our celebrating is magnified. An angel at the top of our Christmas tree is precious not only because it was made by a beloved aunt and has graced the tree for years, but also because it links us with the joyous message of those first angelic visitors who announced the birth of the Saviour. A christening gown is special not only because it was worn by grandpa and great-grandma, but also because for generations the newly baptized have worn white garments as a symbol of the new life they have entered into.

Some of us may not recall such objects in our homes. Perhaps in our families, it was special places or favorite stories or jokes that evoked a sense of continuity. For other families, illness and dysfunction were so great that the only stories told were those of pain and abuse. There is room in God's story of redemption for even those difficult stories to find expression and healing, and for new patterns of celebration to be nurtured.

Your particular family style of celebrating is a matter of taste and tradition, just as some prefer to worship in a plain meeting room and others in a cathedral. The important thing is that everyone be included in the shaping of the celebration, that the story or the event be made our own, and that whether fancy and formal or spontaneous and low-key, there be a sense of purpose that points to the presence of God in our midst as being the true gift that we celebrate.

&

Jesus orchestrated a spontaneous celebration with several of his disciples after he had been resurrected from the dead.

> After this Jesus revealed himself again to the disciples by the Sea of Tiberias; and he revealed himself in this way. Simon Peter, Thomas called the Twin, Nathanael of Cana in Galilee, the sons of Zebedee, and two others of his disciples were together. Simon Peter said to them, "I am going fishing." They said to him, "We will go with you." They went out and got into the boat; but that night they caught nothing.
>
> Just as day was breaking, Jesus stood on the beach; yet the disciples did not know that it was Jesus. Jesus said to them, "Children, have you any fish?" They answered him,

"No." He said to them, "Cast the net on the right side of
the boat, and you will find some." So they cast it, and now
they were not able to haul it in, for the quantity of fish.
That disciple whom Jesus loved said to Peter, "It is the
Lord!" When Simon Peter heard that it was the Lord, he
put on his clothes, for he was stripped for work, and
sprang into the sea. But the other disciples came in the
boat, dragging the net full of fish, for they were not far
from the land, but about a hundred yards off.

When they got out on land, they saw a charcoal fire
there, with fish lying on it, and bread. Jesus said to them,
"Bring some of the fish that you have just caught." So
Simon Peter went aboard and hauled the net ashore, full of
large fish, a hundred and fifty-three of them; and although
there were so many, the net was not torn. Jesus said to
them, "Come and have breakfast." Now none of the
disciples dared ask him, "Who are you?" They knew it
was the Lord. Jesus came and took the bread and gave it to
them, and so with the fish. This was now the third time
that Jesus was revealed to the disciples after he was raised
from the dead.   —John 21:1-14

At the suggestion of Simon Peter, some of the disciples
had gone fishing. Perhaps after the anguish of those last few
days with Jesus before his crucifixion, and then the
astonishing and mysterious appearances that he had made
in their gatherings in Jerusalem, it was comforting to return
to familiar territory and a task that was simple and tangible.

They were fishermen by trade, and they launched out
together for a night of work and camaraderie. But their labor
proved unfruitful. Just as the dawn was breaking and they
were heading into shore, tired, disappointed, and hungry,
their frustration was magnified when they had to answer the
question of a stranger on the shore. No, they had caught
nothing. But there seemed to be a note of authority in the
stranger's voice, so they heeded his suggestion to throw the

net out one more time. After all, the right side *was* the lucky side, and often someone standing on the shore could see a school of fish hidden from the view of those in the boat.

Perhaps the enormous amount of the catch triggered the memory of a previous catch in the mind of John, "the disciple whom Jesus loved." As he peered out through the early morning mist at the figure on shore, John remembered not only the catch that had torn the nets and nearly sunk the boats (Luke 5:6-7), but also the abundance that always seemed to flow whenever Jesus was around—wedding wine in Cana for all the guests, bread for thousands on the hillsides who came to hear his teaching, lively dinner parties in the homes of friends. Suddenly, John knew and he whispered to Peter, "It is the Lord!" Peter took no time to ponder the revelation, but covered himself and sprang into the water to go greet the risen Christ.

What an intimate and memorable celebration that must have been! While it came as quite a surprise to the wearied disciples, Jesus must have taken some time to prepare the meal, build the fire, clean and cook the fish, secure the bread. With loving attention, he must have stood there tending the fire, watching his friends off in the distance, awaiting their approach. Although Peter was the first to arrive, cold and wet from the sea, Jesus warmly greeted all his disciples and bid them come and eat, inviting them to bring some of their fish to add to the meal.

What memories must have been flooding their hearts as they received the bread and fish from Jesus' own hands—the time that he had fed the 5,000 and had said, "I am the bread of life," the countless meals they had shared together around fires such as this, the last sobering meal they had taken together in the upper room before his death. Their hearts were likely filled with many questions, but they did not ask them, because they knew what was really important—that the risen Lord was with them, the same man who had touched them and walked with them. And that was enough to know, and that was the best reason to celebrate. The one whose very presence seemed to bring an abundance—of wine, bread, fish, living water, eternal life, fullness of the spirit—had given the best gift of all, his presence among them.

How can we recognize and welcome the risen Lord in our own family celebrations? Especially if we are discouraged or tired after a night of frustratingly empty nets, how do we discern his presence calling to us from the shore?

&

We can learn to celebrate Christ's presence in our midst by bringing our family into the church's great story of salvation history—the story of the birth, life, death, and resurrection of Jesus Christ. The church has organized its celebration of these events into two cycles, one that focuses on Christmas and one that focuses on Easter. Each has its own special season of preparation, its own culminating festivities, and its own fulfillment. Each has its own powerful and dramatic story to tell. Our children, indeed all of us, need to celebrate those stories in our homes as well as hear about them in church.

The church year begins with Advent, four Sundays before Christmas. It is a time of cleansing, preparation, and waiting, a time to recall the prophetic messengers who prepared the way for Jesus' first coming and to look ahead toward his coming again. We can tell this story of expectancy and longing as we light Advent candles in our homes, as we thoughtfully and lovingly prepare gifts that share our hearts as well as our money, and as we bring out the crèche figures and journey to Bethlehem with them.

Christmas arrives, and the delight and wonder of giving and receiving gifts, of feasting and singing, should be seen as a small attempt to point us to the extravagance of God's gift to us in the Christ child. It is a twelve-day feast that concludes with the celebration of Epiphany on January sixth, commemorating the arrival of the wise men and the sharing of the light of Christ with all of the world.

We can tell the story differently in the late winter and spring during the Lent and Easter cycle. Lent begins in the dead of winter with the stark reminder of our mortality, the act of putting ashes on our foreheads on Ash Wednesday. We can speak of cleansing and preparation as we simplify our eating during Lent, or perhaps do a spring cleaning and give away possessions that are cluttering our lives. We can plant seeds deep in the ground and watch things grow as we speak of the one who spent three days in the dark grave and then was transformed. We can carry home our processional palms from the church's celebration of Palm Sunday and weave them into crosses. As we dye and hide our Easter eggs, we can contemplate the bright glory of the new life that the hope of the resurrection brings. Easter is a forty-day season, a time to tell and ponder the stories of Jesus' resurrection appearances, a time to celebrate spring and the abundance of new life. It concludes with Ascension and then Pentecost, the sharing of the story of new life with all the peoples of the earth.

For some, these home celebrations may be quite elaborate and formal—a family devotional time around the Advent candles, special songs and readings, meatless meals during Lent, a Last Supper Passover meal. For others, the celebrations will be less structured—a spur-of-the-moment drive through the neighborhood to marvel at the Christmas lights, carolling in the homes of shut-ins, an impromptu Palm Sunday parade around the backyard. But whatever style suits the personality of our family, in each celebration we have the opportunity to recognize and welcome the presence of Christ, by receiving his joy, by including everyone in the preparations, and by letting the story of Jesus find words in our lives.

Besides the great liturgical cycles of Christmas and Easter, our lives are filled with more personal celebrations, such as birthdays and anniversaries, homecomings and departures, baptisms and graduations, promotions and retirements. We can invite Christ in to these special moments as we cherish each individual in the family for his or her uniqueness and delight in the gifts that we are to one another.

During his time on this earth, Jesus was known for his ability to have a good time with all kinds of people. He enjoyed dinner parties and sought out special friends who offered him hospitality. He can be among us as we think of creative ways to honor those in our families for the special events that have meaning in their lives. He brings our story into his own and gives it fresh meaning as he is invited into those pivotal points in our lives.

There will be times when Jesus' story seems very far from our own—when we have to wrestle the kids down for bedtime prayers because they are wild and rambunctious and not at all interested; when we carefully bring home the palm branches from church on Palm Sunday to fashion palm crosses, only to find our children racing through the house and using the palms as weapons with which to whack each other over the head; when we have lost the baby Jesus from our ornately carved nativity set and spend the rest of Advent wondering where he is.

Jesus calls us, even then, to still come and be a part of *his* story, *his* celebration. He calls us through the morning mist, after a night of discouragement, to come have breakfast with him, to partake of the feast he has been preparing all along.

&

When Jesus was a boy, his senses must have been filled with the scents and sounds and sights of celebration. Perhaps the first prayers he experienced were those of his mother as she lighted the Sabbath lamps and those of his father as he said the blessing over the wine and bread. Maybe his mother made a little loaf of the finest Sabbath bread just for him, so that he could follow after his father, saying the special blessing.

Mary and Joseph must have been faithful in telling him the story of God's saving acts throughout their people's history. With candles and spices, *matzoth* and wine, with pilgrimages to Jerusalem and walks down the block to the synagogue, with lullabies and lessons, legends and interpretations, they celebrated the story of God's infinite love for his people and his promises to send the Messiah.

As a man, he certainly knew the Sabbath as a good and abundant gift to be cherished, as an opportunity to bring life and healing. The stories, the songs, the feasting, the welcoming of friends, must have all shaped his early years.

He must have felt included, welcomed and truly a part of God's story, for when he was grown he certainly knew how to welcome all sorts who came to him, from the blind beggar to the secretive Pharisee, from the child to the Roman soldier.

Jesus lived and breathed the story. It became his own. He gave it flesh as did no other before or after.

Because Mary and Joseph took the time and energy to include Jesus in the rhythm of their life with God, he had the opportunity to learn, embrace, and celebrate that story. As

they passed on the wonder and joy of God's saving events to
their little boy, so we have the opportunity to be caught up
in God's saving story and to celebrate God's presence with
us.

Epilogue

EACH NEW STAGE IN THE LIFE OF OUR FAMILY challenges us to face our own inadequacies and turn to God with renewed desire to receive the grace to let go and learn new things.

We parents have the tendency to want to "arrive," to learn the right things to stay in control. If we take the right childbirth class and practice the breathing, then we will be able to *handle* labor. If we read the right books and buy the right potty seat, we should be able to deal with toilet training. If we start saving now, college tuition should not come as such a shock. But our children seldom allow us to stay in control.

We remember good friends visiting us in the hospital shortly after the premature labor had been stopped during our first pregnancy. "This is just the first of many crises you will be facing as parents." Having nearly lost our baby, we felt this comment was a bit flip, but through the years, when we are especially feeling out of control, we think back to that day and smile at how very true that comment was.

What a gift our children bring in revealing to us again and again that we cannot be in control, that we have not arrived. Being faithful Christian parents is not something that we master by reading a book or learning some techniques. We become faithful Christian parents by becoming faithful Christians, by daily opening our hearts to walk with the One who longs to take on flesh and blood in us.

And that is a process that never ends. John has a song called *The Journey Never Ends*, we leave you with its chorus:

> The journey never ends.
> No, the journey never ends
> Until the day the kingdom comes,
> Until the day our lovemaking
> Never comes undone.

May God pour out much laughter, patience, and love upon us all, parents and children alike, as we open our hearts to grace and welcome his lively presence into our families.

About the Authors

BETSY DAWN INSKEEP SMYLIE is Missioner to the Deaf and Vicar of Ephphatha Church of the Deaf in Western, New York. She is a graduate of Radcliffe and Harvard Divinity School and her writing has appeared in a variety of magazines and journals as well as a weekly newspaper column.

JOHN SHERIDAN SMYLIE is Rector of Trinity Church of Hamburg, New York. He was educated at Syracuse University and Episcopal Divinity School. He is an accomplished singer and songwriter and performs concerts in a variety of settings and venues in addition to his work as a parish priest.

The Smylies live in Orchard Park, New York with their two children.